TRAIN UP A Mom

a Bible Study for Mothers

VOLLIE SANDERS

NAVPRESS
BRINGING TRUTH TO LIFE
NavPress Publishing Group
P.O. Box 35001, Colorado Springs, Colorado 80935

OUR GUARANTEE TO YOU

We believe so strongly in the message of our books that we are making this quality guarantee to you. If for any reason you are disappointed with the content of this book, return the title page to us with your name and address and we will refund to you the list price of the book. To help us serve you better, please briefly describe why you were disappointed. Mail your refund request to: NavPress, P.O. Box 35002, Colorado Springs, CO 80935.

The Navigators is an international Christian organization. Our mission is to reach, disciple, and equip people to know Christ and to make Him known through successive generations. We envision multitudes of diverse people in the United States and every other nation who have a passionate love for Christ, live a lifestyle of sharing Christ's love, and multiply spiritual laborers among those without Christ.

NavPress is the publishing ministry of The Navigators. NavPress publications help believers learn biblical truth and apply what they learn to their lives and ministries. Our mission is to stimulate spiritual formation among our readers.

© 1997 by Vollie Sanders

ISBN 1-57683-002-0

Cover Photo: Ariel Skelley

Some of the anecdotal illustrations in this book are true to life and are included with the permission of the persons involved. All other illustrations are composites of real situations, and any resemblance to people living or dead is coincidental.

Unless otherwise identified, all Scripture quotations in this publication are taken from the *HOLY BIBLE: NEW INTERNATIONAL VERSION* ® (NIV®). Copyright © 1973, 1978, 1984 by International Bible Society. Used by permission of Zondervan Publishing House. All rights reserved. Other versions used include: the *New American Standard Bible* (NASB), © The Lockman Foundation 1960, 1962, 1963, 1968, 1971, 1972, 1973, 1975, 1977; *The Message: New Testament with Psalms and Proverbs* by Eugene H. Peterson, copyright © 1993, 1994, 1995, used by permission of NavPress Publishing Group; *The New Testament in Modern English* (PH), J. B. Phillips Translator, © J. B. Phillips 1958, 1960, 1972, used by permission of Macmillan Publishing Company; *The Living Bible* (TLB), copyright © 1971, used by permission of Tyndale House Publishers, Inc., Wheaton, IL 60189, all rights reserved; the *Amplified New Testament* (AMP), © The Lockman Foundation 1954, 1958; and the *New King James Version* (NKJV), copyright © 1979, 1980, 1982, 1990, Thomas Nelson Inc., Publishers.

Printed in the United States of America

5 6 7 8 9 10 11 12 13 14 15 16 / 06 05 04 03 02

FOR A FREE CATALOG OF
NAVPRESS BOOKS & BIBLE STUDIES,
CALL 1-800-366-7788 (USA)
OR 1-416-499-4615 (CANADA)

Contents

Acknowledgments

This study is designed specifically for mothers. But the content is full of a lifetime of input, guidance, and encouragement given to me by my husband of almost forty years. Without him I never would have attempted this desire of my heart, a Bible study teaching women to look to God for direction in raising their children.

I must also thank many close friends who encouraged me in my pursuit through much prayer, helping with computer skills, and many hours of rewrites. Many provided words of strength to my soul when I was discouraged and ready to quit.

I am also grateful to my children. Without their willingness for me to share stories from their lives, you would not understand how God has worked through their parents' lives as we raised them up for His glory.

Then, most of all, rich praise to our God for His faithfulness to me over the years of walking with Him. This study is written so that all mothers will bring praise to His name as they walk through the raising of their children.

Preface

❧

"Train up a child in the way he should go; and when he is old, he will not depart from it," reads Proverbs 22:6, KJV. This verse has been foundational for many parents, from the births of their children through adulthood, and for some even through the deaths of their children. My husband and I used to think that no matter what happens, this verse will somehow always work for parents.

After many years of attempting to find security in this verse, I realized I had no idea what it meant! I did not really understand the verse when I looked at all the contradictions in my own children and others. At that point, I wasn't sure that I believed it!

I had many questions about the meaning of the verse. For example, how *old* would my children have to be before they walked in God's way? Sometimes I had seen children walk with Him in their youth and turn away in their teens. How was I to know the *right* way to direct my children, and what if they refused to go the way I thought best?

I also struggled with the word *train*. Did this mean that regular attendance at church and religious activities would ensure they would live God's way? Was this what training meant? Would these things make them hungry for our invisible God?

After honestly facing these questions, I finally realized the person who really needed the training was me—their mother! I needed to assure my own heart that God had led me in the way He intended me to go. When I began to allow the Lord to teach me how to desire Him, how to trust and to walk with Him, it became much easier to entrust my children to Him.

When I involved myself in the study of His Word, I began to learn how God Himself trains His children. I learned how He responds to His children when they fail, how He perseveres and continues to lead them forward to His plan. Through this studying I began to understand Proverbs 22:6. The same principles that apply to God's training of me also apply to my training of my children. And God trains me as I trust Him to guide me in training them.

This Bible study does not promise answers to all problems and questions involved in raising children. It will enable you to walk with and look to God for answers as you apply the principles. Some readers may feel it is too late, but our Lord is a God of hope and a God of miracles. I have experienced this in my own life and my children's lives. It is my prayer this will be a catalyst in helping you walk intimately with God through all the years He entrusts you with children. When you begin to study your children, to pray for them, to claim promises for them, to surrender them, you will reflect the Lord to them—and to others also.

As you involve yourself in these studies, you will realize that the training of children *and* of mothers never stops. I enjoy using these principles as I pray for my grown children and grandchildren. It is a lifelong process of believing God to show us His way for them. You will join the ranks of those mentioned in Hebrews 11:6: "And without faith it is impossible to please Him, for he who comes to God must believe that He is, and that He is a rewarder of those who seek Him" (NASB).

May God help, bless, and instruct you in His ways, as you trust Him to train your precious children.

VOLLIE SANDERS

Lead the Way

How shall I lead my child?
In the way that he should go, said Solomon.
Do I know the Way?
What shall I teach my child?
Of the true God, said Moses.
Do I know the Truth?
I want my child to have life.
He who has the Son has Life, said John.
Do I have Life?
I cannot lead my child
Unless I know the Way . . .
I cannot speak of Truth
Unless I know It . . .
I cannot tell my child of Life
Unless I have It.
Jesus is The Way
The Truth
The Life. . . .
It is in knowing Him . . . that I find the way to lead my child.

RODLYN DANOS[1]

To Want to Grow

*You, however, continue in the things you have learned and
become convinced of, knowing from whom you have
learned them; and that from childhood you have known the
sacred writings which are able to give you the wisdom that
leads to salvation through faith which is in Christ Jesus.*
2 TIMOTHY 3:14-15, NASB

[Christ] wants a child's heart, but a grown-up's head.
He wants us to be simple, single-minded, affectionate,
and teachable, as good children are; but He also wants every
bit of intelligence we have to be alert at its job,
and in first-class fighting trim.
C. S. LEWIS, *MERE CHRISTIANITY*[1]

I started my training as a very young mother, away from my family, and without having a relationship with Jesus Christ. Although I had some baby-sitting experience as a teenager, even knowing how to hold this tiny child was something entirely foreign to me. I needed training in all areas, even basic physical care.

It was not until much later that I began to understand that physical care would never be enough to raise my child. After all, far more is involved in training a child than merely knowing how to meet physical needs. There are emotional, mental, social, and spiritual needs—areas that I didn't even understand in my own life—and I knew much less about how to train my child in the right ways. Even after committing my life to Christ, I realized how much more I had to learn. How much did I really understand about the *way* to walk with Christ, the *truth* that Christ offered, or how to experience *life* as defined in His Word? When my baby cried all day and night, how would I handle the anger and the tiredness that threatened to overwhelm me? When my two-year-old said "No!" for the twentieth time in two hours, how would I control my spirit, keeping her interests at heart and not my own comfort, as I helped her obey? When I did not like my teenager, how would I continue to love her and to walk by faith and hope in God? How could I believe in the character and goodness of God rather than yielding to the overwhelming fear for my children's future? It was obvious that I needed training!

Why Moms Need Training

Rebekah, Isaac's wife, longed to have children. After years of barrenness and much prayer, she became pregnant with twin sons: Esau and Jacob. As the firstborn, Esau was entitled to the greater inheritance and his father's deathbed blessing. But Rebekah developed a favorite among her two sons: the second-born Jacob. She began to plan how to accomplish her dreams for his future.

1. As you read Genesis 27:1-17, think about Rebekah's choices and the results.

   a. How did Rebekah respond when she discovered her husband was dying? What specific decision did she make?

   b. Why do you think she made these choices?

   c. What principles was she teaching her son by her actions?

   d. How did Rebekah demonstrate she had no concern for God's plan or any desire to obey Him?

Rebekah's plan worked perfectly; she got what she wanted for her favorite son!

2. Read Genesis 27:41-45. Write down the results of Rebekah's plan as recorded in the passage.

Results for herself

Results for her sons

3. As you think about Rebekah and her choices, do you find yourself identifying with her desires to give her child a future hope? What do you think you would have done in these circumstances?

How should a relationship with God affect the way we view the circumstances of life? Rebekah was confronted with her own selfish desire for her son. She did not seem to feel that what God was allowing could possibly be the best for him. *She needed training!* God was attempting to help her believe Him by faith, even though the circumstances were leading to exactly the opposite of what she wanted for Jacob. God was trying to help Rebekah love her child in the way that He loves: *He always looks out for the child's best interest and His purpose for the child.* God wanted Rebekah to let Him have His way to direct her son, rather than using all of her power as a mother to get her way.

༄

Five I have; each separate, distinct, a soul bound for eternity:
and I . . . blind leader of the blind . . . groping and fumbling, casual and concerned by turns. . . .

Undisciplined, I seek by order and command to
discipline and shape;
(I who need Thy discipline to shape my own
disordered soul).
O Thou who seest the heart's true, deep desire, each
shortcoming
and each sad mistake, supplement and overrule,
nor let our children be the victims of our own
unlikeness unto Thee.

RUTH BELL GRAHAM, *Sitting by My Laughing Fireplace*[2]

A young mother shared that she had no idea how selfish she was until she had her first child! Most of our training as mothers involves finding out how far away we are from what God intends us to be as His children. Matthew 5:48 says, "Therefore you are to be perfect, as your heavenly Father is perfect" (NASB).

As we begin to recognize the difference between our lives and God's standards, we can be encouraged that He is committed to helping us become like Him. *Our part* in this change process is to choose to respond in obedience to Him in whatever He allows in our lives. *God's part* is based on His commitment to us because of the relationship we have with His Son and because of His great love for us.

4. Meditate on the following passage:

In face of all this, what is there left to say? If God is for us, who can be against us? He who did not grudge His own Son but gave Him up for us all—can we not trust such a God to give us, with Him, everything else that we can need?

Who would dare accuse us, whom God has chosen? The judge Himself has declared us free from sin. Who is in a position to condemn? Only Christ, and Christ died for us, Christ rose for us, Christ reigns in power for us, Christ prays for us!

Who can separate us from the love of Christ? Can trouble, pain or persecution? Can lack of clothes and food, danger to life and limb, the threat of force of arms? . . . No, in all these things we win an overwhelming victory through Him who has proved His love for us. (Romans 8:31-37, PH)

a. From this passage, list the things God has promised to do in your life.

b. In which of these areas do you have the most difficulty believing God?

c. As you believe God in that area, how do you expect you will experience His blessing?

Training is for Moms

Moses, who led the Hebrews out of slavery in Egypt, had a younger man named Joshua as a helper. He had been with Moses all through the years when the people wandered in the wilderness because of their rebellion. Joshua had been faithful and obedient to what Moses said to do. When Moses died, God commissioned Joshua to take his place and lead the people. Moses had been training this young man all through the wilderness years, allowing him to see success and failure as he led the people. When God gave this responsibility to Joshua, He spoke about specific priorities, values, and attitudes that a man *or woman* of God should embrace.

5. Look at Joshua 1:1-9 and list the statements about Joshua that apply under each of the following sections.

The *priorities* (most important tasks and goals)[3] that God wanted Joshua to pursue:

The *values* (principles or moral standards)[4] that God wanted Joshua to live by:

The *attitudes* (ways of acting, feeling, or thinking that show one's disposition or opinion)[5] that God wanted Joshua to display:

6. Why do you think God repeated in verses 7 and 9 His instruction to be strong and courageous?

7. What specific promise did God give Joshua in verses 5 and 9?

8. How does this passage apply to your life as you raise your children?

God told Joshua that his success and prosperity depended upon his meditating on "this Book of the Law" day and night (verse 8). For Joshua, "this Book of the Law" meant Genesis through Deuteronomy, since that was all of the Bible that existed in his day. For us the "book" includes the rest of the Bible as well.

9. Why do you think the priority of studying the Bible is a criterion for success and prosperity?

The success and prosperity mentioned in Joshua 1 have to do with the recognition that, in our own abilities, we cannot accomplish the mission God has given us as believers. Our success and prosperity come from dependence on and an understanding of His Word. Applying the Word to our lives causes us to change and grow, no matter how old we become.

Read the following verse. Use it to meditate as you ponder your need for training in these areas.

Faithful is He who calls you, and He also will bring it to pass. (1 Thessalonians 5:24, NASB)

A Mom's Memory

Obedience! That was my topic for an upcoming women's retreat, but I seemed to have trouble getting everyone else in my home to cooperate with my goals. Having just returned from the Christmas holidays, I had unpacking and washing to do, a house full of people, decorations to put away, cookies to bake for the retreat, unhappy children—even the dog seemed to need my attention. As I wrote down the first profound thought for my talk on obedience, I smelled the cookies burning and heard the sound of a waterfall in the laundry room. I ignored the cookies and ran into the laundry room to find the water pipes had frozen and burst. Water was pouring all over everything. As my children and the dog watched, I yelled, "Lord, how do you expect me to learn anything about obedience with all this happening?"

During the next few hours, my children learned more about obedience than through all the sermons I had ever delivered. They watched as I struggled to obey God in my circumstances. Did I really believe that "in all things God works for the good of those who love him, who have been called according to his purpose" (Romans 8:28)? Would I really be able to "give thanks in all circumstances" (1 Thessalonians 5:18)? Just as God knew about Joshua, my children fully knew their mom and how much she needed God's help to learn about obedience.

Just like Joshua, you and I need training. God was faithful to train me in the realities of obedience in a way I would never have planned. He revealed to me and to my children my desperate need of Him. Most of our training to be moms involves learning that we really can't do this job of training our children alone. *God* has to be our trainer as well.

At the very end of his life, the apostle Paul understood that training would always be a part of a believer's life. Read his words. Meditate and pray that God would keep this attitude of foward growth uppermost in your mind as you continue this study.

Yet my brothers, I do not consider myself to have arrived spiritually, nor do I consider myself already perfect. But I keep going on, grasping ever more firmly that purpose for which Christ Jesus grasped me. My brothers, I do not consider myself to have fully grasped it even now. But I do concentrate on this: I leave the past behind and with hands outstretched to whatever lies ahead I go straight for the goal . . . my reward the honour of my high calling by God in Christ Jesus.

PHILIPPIANS 3:12-14, PII

For Personal Meditation

10. a. Are you willing to commit yourself to the lifelong process of growth? Why or why not?

   b. From this chapter, what have you understood to be your purpose as a mother?

   c. Are you willing to leave the past and reach toward the future God has planned for you? How will you do that?

At the end of Paul's life, he still felt inadequate for the task God had given him, yet his determined purpose was to keep reaching for God's best. This study recognizes that growth is a lifelong process; it will continue until we are perfected in Him. As we continue this study, addressing the *whys* and *whats* of training moms, I pray that you will meet God in a new way as *He* trains you in His ways.

For Personal Prayer
Ask God to keep you eagerly growing in your knowledge of Him and His ways in order to faithfully pass this desire on to your children.

Two
TRAIN UP A MOM:
To Walk in Intimacy

~

And I pray that you, firmly fixed in love yourselves, may be able to grasp (with all Christians) how wide and deep and long and high is the love of Christ . . . and to know for yourselves that love so far beyond our comprehension. May you be filled through all your being with God Himself.

EPHESIANS 3:17-19, PH

Having the reality of God's presence is not dependent on our being in a particular circumstance or place, but it is dependent on our determination to keep the Lord before us continually. Our problems arise when we refuse to place our trust in the reality of His presence.

OSWALD CHAMBERS, *My Utmost for His Highest*[1]

For many years I saw God as the grandfather in the sky. He was the One I called on when I was in trouble or when I wanted something. Apart from that, I didn't seem to need Him for anything else, and I didn't want or desire His interference in my daily affairs.

Then I was brought face to face with someone who had an intimate relationship with Him: my husband. The hunger for Christ I saw in his life made me realize I had never experienced that kind of close relationship with God. I probably knew more about the Bible than my husband, but I did not know the Author in the way that he did—intimately!

God's Call to Intimacy

1. a. According to the following passages, how does God demonstrate His love for you through His actions?
   Psalm 103:1-5

   Psalm 18:16-19

   Romans 8:38-39

   1 John 4:9-10,19

   b. Which of these verses means the most to you? Explain your answer.

2. Read Psalm 103:8-14.

   a. Describe the attitudes God demonstrates toward His children.

   b. As a mother, which of these attitudes do you find most difficult to demonstrate toward your children?

   c. Look up the word *compassion* in a dictionary. Describe a time when God showed compassion to you.

d. According to the verses, why do you think God shows such great compassion toward His children?

3. Read Matthew 11:28-30.

a. What is Jesus asking us to do in these verses?

b. Why do you think mothers especially need to go to Jesus?

c. Why do you think Jesus mentions His gentleness and humility as qualifications for giving you the rest you seek?

d. When has God given you *rest for your soul?* Be specific.

A Mom's Memory

I remember the first time I read these penetrating words Jesus spoke to Philip, one of His disciples: "Have I been so long with you, and yet you have not come to know Me, Philip?" (John 14:8, NASB) Immediately I felt great sorrow because I knew Jesus was asking that question of me; He was putting my own name in the place of *Philip!*

Like Philip, I had known about Jesus for a long time, but I had never fully realized His great love for me. I had read the Bible, His love letter to me, but paid little attention to what He was telling me about Himself or about the meaning of life. What a loving God! He continued to pursue me even when I was paying no attention to Him!

Our Response to Intimacy

4. Get to know Zacchaeus by reading Luke 19:1-10. Then answer the following questions.

    a. What was Zacchaeus looking for?

    b. What obstacles prevented him from finding the intimacy he desired?

    c. How did the Lord respond to Zacchaeus?

    d. And how did Zacchaeus respond to the opportunity to meet Jesus?

Busy mothers often don't respond to the opportunities to meet Jesus in the same way Zacchaeus did because we let other things take priority. In fact, sometimes we don't seem to have even a spare moment for ourselves. With two teenagers and a new baby, I often found myself in that situation. Sometimes when it became obvious to everyone that I was at the end of my rope, my dear husband would send me upstairs to be alone. The objective was for me to do whatever I needed most . . . sleep, spend time with the Lord, or tend to a project that required attention.

But other things seemed to interfere. When I tried to sleep, I felt guilty that I wasn't spending time with the Lord. If I spent time with Him in the Word, I felt guilty that I wasn't getting the rest I needed. I wasted away most of the time listening to the noises downstairs and wondering if my husband was handling things the "right" way. Consequently, I found *no rest for my soul* even when I had the opportunity.

I finally realized that I had to choose to respond to God as I made decisions about how to use the time He gave me. I also had to recognize that I had a faithful enemy, *Satan,* who did not want me to involve Jesus in my everyday life and who would do everything to prevent that. At that moment, I decided to choose—again and again throughout my days—to involve Jesus, no matter what I was doing. He was always there beside me if I would only recognize His presence.

☙

Alone, O Lord, alone with Thee,
Where none could speak nor hear nor see,
the bar I placed across my heart
I'd lift and bid the doors to part . . .
on rusty wings open wide
And let just once your love inside.
And when I'd turn to close the door
And put the bar in place once more . . .
My heart so filled with Thee I'd find
The doors could not be closed behind.
SHIRLEY GUPTON LYNN, FROM *For Everything There is a Season*[2]

☙

5. As you consider choosing to involve Jesus in everything you do as a mom, answer the following questions.

a. What are some things that keep you from establishing an intimate relationship with Jesus?

b. What choices will you make today to begin to respond to Jesus? What, for instance, will you do to remove the roadblocks you just identified?

A Pattern for Intimacy

In John 13:23, the writer refers to himself as "the disciple whom Jesus loved." Since there is nothing to indicate that Jesus loved John more than anyone else, I decided also to become the disciple whom Jesus loved. Now when I come before the Lord to meet with Him each day, I greet Him with these words: "This is Vollie, Your beloved disciple." Immediately I feel loved and accepted by Him.

6. In order to practice building intimacy with the Lord, you first need to get set up.

Equipment: Gather your Bible, some paper, a pen, and — if required to function — coffee. I like to use a notebook or journal to record my thoughts so I can have a record of God's communication with me.
Time: I prefer the morning, but find a time that works for you.
Place: Go to a place where you can be alone for a few minutes.

To begin, choose a small portion of Scripture. I would suggest starting at the beginning of one of the gospels, perhaps Mark 1:1-8. (I generally follow the natural breaks in my Bible to determine the length of the passage I'm studying each day.) Think about the following questions and, after dating your entry, write as much as you can in response to each.

a. What is happening in this passage? And what is the context of that event?
b. What action, attitude, and/or relationship is presented in the passage?
c. What do these observations have to do with my life today?

No matter how much time you have for your journal, use the first person ("I," "me") when you write so you are able to be intimate and personal with God. Then, as you finish your time with Him, pray and ask Him to remind you all day of the things you have learned in His Word and how He would have those words affect your thinking as you walk through His plan for your life that day.

❧

"We are as close to God as we CHOOSE to be . . . not as we WANT to be; but as we CHOOSE to be!"

J. OSWALD SANDERS[3]

❧

Intimacy with the Lord is not just setting aside time to read your Bible and pray. It is being in a relationship with Him that continues throughout the day and night. The pattern I have suggested for spending time with Him can help you build this habit into your life. And that habit can change your life in both big ways and small as you learn to call on God throughout the day.

Early one morning, for instance, I read these words from Isaiah 26:20 before anyone woke up:

> Come, my people, enter into your rooms,
> And close your doors behind you;
> Hide for a little while,
> Until indignation runs its course.... (NASB)

Later that day when life was overwhelming me, I ran to my only private place—the bathroom!—and hid there with the Lord until He calmed me with His presence. After that time of hiding with Him, I was able to face what He was allowing in my life that day.

Recently when our grown children wrote individual love letters to my husband and me, sharing memories from their childhood, I saw what an impact my regular times with the Lord had on them. One daughter wrote, "I remember you spending time praying and developing your relationship with the Lord each day. I didn't really understand it then, but I surely do now." Now, as the mother of three children, she understands that her lifework of child-rearing can't be accomplished without a deep relationship with Christ.

For Personal Meditation

7. Hear Jesus' love for you in Revelation 3:20 and then consider the questions that follow.

"Behold, I stand at the door and knock; if anyone hears My voice and opens the door, I will come in to him, and will dine with him, and he with Me." (NASB)

a. Are you certain you have a personal relationship with Jesus Christ? How and when did this relationship start?
b. What must you do to increase your intimacy with this God who loves you? Be specific about your goal and how you plan to reach that goal.
c. What courageous first step should you take today?

8. Review the following steps to intimacy:

    ‿Determine that you will meet with God sometime during each day.
    ‿Don't give up. Tomorrow is a new beginning.
    ‿Enlist the help of a friend. Swap childcare time so you can each have time alone.
    ‿If you are a nursing mother, use that time to pray a special verse for your child. (Psalm 138:8 is a favorite verse for me.)
    ‿Share what God is saying to you with your children, your husband, or a friend. Don't preach but share the joy of meeting with Him.

Everything in your Christian life, everything about knowing Him and experiencing Him, everything about knowing His will, depends on the quality of your love relationship to God.
HENRY T. BLACKABY AND CLAUDE V. KING, *Experiencing God*[4]

For Personal Prayer

Write a brief prayer committing yourself to growing in intimacy with your heavenly Father.

TRAIN UP A MOM:
To Accept God's Way

For we are His workmanship, created in Christ Jesus for good works, which God prepared beforehand, that we should walk in them.
EPHESIANS 2:10, NASB

God has set out a plan that is moving under His perfect direction. Wise is the parent who cooperates with that plan. It takes prayer. It takes time with God. It takes concentration. It takes thought. It takes observation. It takes caring. And it takes communication. It also takes watching reactions and responding when the reaction comes.
CHARLES R. SWINDOLL, *Growing Wise in Family Life*[1]

God knows everything about your children. Nothing that touches them is a surprise to Him. Does this give you reassurance when you face something unexpected—or do you feel threatened by that truth? Perhaps your child was born with some difficult problems and the joy you anticipated has turned into unending and unanswerable questions. Perhaps the trouble came later when, as adolescents, your children seemed to turn away from all of your dreams and plans for their lives. Wherever your children are today, God isn't surprised, and He hasn't stopped loving them or being active in their lives.

A large part of our training as mothers involves learning to accept God's loving control over the circumstances He allows in our children's lives. A child's personality, physical appearance, responsiveness to God and to us—all the traits that make that child who he is—were known and planned by God, and He will use them specifically for your training. These unique *identification marks* make each child very special to God. There is no one else like that child for Him to love.

Accepting God's Handiwork

1. Referring to the following Scriptures, list the things God knew about your children before their births.

   Psalm 139:1-3

   Psalm 139:4-5

   Psalm 139:7-12

   Psalm 139:13-16

2. What does God reveal in the verses that follow about His desire to do good for your child(ren)?

   Psalm 139:17-18

   Jeremiah 29:11

   Isaiah 54:10

   2 Corinthians 5:21

3. Pause to think about your child(ren) as God's handiwork and answer these questions:

   a. What about your child/each of your children is unique?

   b. What are you doing to respond sensitively and wisely to these unique qualities that you see in your child?

   c. Are you willing to cooperate with God in the training of your child(ren) for His glory? Why or why not?

   d. Have you fully accepted your child(ren) as the handiwork of God? Using a scale of 1 to 5, with 5 being "completely and wholeheartedly," indicate in the chart below how fully you have accepted each aspect of each of your children's lives.

Name	Physical	Mental	Social	Spiritual

*Ruth Bell Graham always asked this question when dealing
with her children: How has God dealt with me? She believed
God was working on her just as hard as she was working on
her children. She could only change herself and become an
example instead of a judge. From time-to-time each day she
needed to sit down and indulge herself in the Lord to renew her
perspective.*

PATRICIA DANIELS CORNWELL,
Time for Remembering, The Story of Ruth Bell Graham[2]

Accepting God's Purpose

4. The gospel of Luke tells the miraculous story of the angel Gabriel's
visit to Mary when he told her that she had been chosen to be the
mother of God's Son. Read this prophecy in Luke 1:26-38 and answer
the following questions. Note the verses where you found the
answers.

a. What did the angel tell Mary about the baby, and what titles did he
give to this unique child?

b. What did the angel say God would do?

c. What was Mary's response to this word from God?

d. How do you think Mary felt about this honor given her?

According to the Law of Moses, each baby boy born in a Jewish
family had to be circumcised and presented to the Lord in the temple.
When Mary and Joseph took Jesus to the temple with the prescribed

offerings, they were met by a man named Simeon who offered another prophecy concerning their son.

5. Read Luke 2:25-35.

   a. What does Luke tell us about Simeon?

   b. Why was Simeon in the temple?

   c. What happened when Simeon saw Jesus?

   d. What did Simeon prophesy for this child and His mother Mary?

   e. How do you think Mary felt when she heard these words?

6. It's not hard to know which of these two prophecies — Gabriel's or Simeon's — we would most like for our children! But it's inevitable that our children will know pain in this life.

   a. What happens in your heart when you hear that difficulties have come to your children?

   b. Where do you take your fears?

A Mom's Memory

Little Judy was born into our family when I was five. She smiled, recognized people, and loved hamburgers. But because of a birth injury, she never walked or talked or even sat up without being tied to her special chair. In spite of going to faith healers and many doctors, my parents saw only a worsening of her condition, and Judy died at age 10. But with Judy's entrance into our lives, my parents, my younger sister, and I were forever changed. Although her time with us was incredibly difficult for my parents, we all found great joy in the "special" child. Along with some measure of success, we also knew growth, sorrow, failure, and shame as we responded to Judy's condition.

How was God's purpose served through this child? Why did He allow her to be injured at birth? I have no answer to those questions. But I do know that God trained us all through her short life, and His lessons are evident in our response to those in similar circumstances. The desire of our hearts is for them to experience the good God can bring from life's difficulties and to show them we understand their struggles. We have an intense longing to see little Judy in heaven, standing *perfect* before our Lord God.

Sometimes God's plans and purposes, and the questions behind them, have to be explained by Him alone. When we moms begin dreaming about our children before they are born, our plans don't usually include pain or sorrow. Instead, we dream about what appears to us to be good for them. Our full acceptance of the fact that, in God's redemptive hands, hard things may bring good results to our children can come only when we are walking closely with Him.

"For My thoughts are not your thoughts,
Neither are your ways My ways," declares the LORD.
"For as the heavens are higher than the earth,
So are My ways higher than your ways,
And My thoughts than your thoughts."
ISAIAH 55:8-9, NASB

Accepting God's Plan

Jacob had many sons, but it was no secret that Joseph was his favorite. Very jealous of their favored brother, Joseph's older brothers sold him into slavery in Egypt and made it look to Jacob as if a wild beast had devoured his youngest son. After many years, and many difficulties for Joseph, the Egyptian pharaoh put him in charge of the land. When famine struck the Middle East, the pharaoh gave him the responsibility of distributing food. Joseph's brothers, not realizing that he was still alive, went to Egypt to obtain food for their families. They did not know that the man they approached was the brother they had sold into slavery.

7. Read Genesis 45:1-8 and 50:15-21.

    a. What was Joseph's attitude toward his brothers?

    b. Why does Joseph say God allowed these things to happen to him?

    c. When they realized who he was, what response do you think Joseph's brothers expected from him?

    d. Why do you think Joseph was able to respond to his brothers the way that he did?

    e. What are some of the character qualities God can build in our lives as a result of suffering?

    f. If Joseph were your son, how do you think you would have felt about and responded to the things God allowed in his life?

Sometimes in the midst of difficult circumstances we may feel that God has forgotten His good plan for our children. Surely Joseph's parents didn't see anything *good* in the loss of their son. But God's plan, unseen and misunderstood by everyone involved, was moving forward. Even before Joseph's birth, God had been at work preparing a place of service for Joseph and giving him unique talents, gifts, and qualities so he would fit into His plan to deliver the Jews from the famine. Then, as Joseph grew, God fit him for the task by building endurance, faith, and integrity in his life. Though most of the afflictions in his life were caused by the unfair treatment of others, Joseph humbly turned to God for help and hope. He accepted the events of his life as coming from the hand of God and as being in line with God's ultimate purpose for his life.

As mothers, we may not always have a Joseph for a son. But regardless of our children and their responses to God, we must accept God's way of training them up. We must embrace His plan for them even though we may find it hard to understand. This acceptance enables us to rest in His unfailing love as He continues to train us as well.

⟨❧⟩

Certainty is the mark of the commonsense life . . . gracious uncertainty is the mark of the spiritual life. To be certain of God means that we are uncertain in all our ways, not knowing what tomorrow may bring. We are uncertain of the next step, but we are certain of God. As soon as we abandon ourselves to God and do the task He has placed closest to us, He begins to fill our lives with His surprises.

OSWALD CHAMBERS, *My Utmost for His Highest*[3]

⟨❧⟩

For Personal Meditation

8. Spend some time reflecting on this verse and then consider the questions that follow.

Trust in the LORD with all your heart,
And do not lean on your own understanding.
In all your ways acknowledge Him,
And He will make your paths straight.
(PROVERBS 3:5-6, NASB)

a. How have you perhaps leaned on your own understanding in making choices for your child? (The consequences of leaning on your own understanding are often not immediately apparent.) What lesson, if any, have you learned from that experience?

b. When have you leaned on your own understanding in accepting or not accepting the circumstances God has allowed in your child's life? (Often, we do not recognize this until later.) What has God said to you about your response to Him?

c. What current choices or circumstances concerning your children are you facing today? What is God asking you to trust Him to do?

For Personal Prayer

Make those situations the topic of prayer right now. Acknowledge God and trust Him to help you believe His goodness in all that you face today.

Four

TRAIN UP A MOM:
To Walk by Faith

*Now faith is being sure of what we hope for
and certain of what we do not see.*
HEBREWS 11:1

True faith depends not upon mysterious signs, celestial
fireworks, or grandiose dispensations from a God who is
seen as a rich, benevolent uncle; true faith as Job
understood, rests on the assurance that God is who He is.
Indeed, on that we must be willing to stake our very lives.
CHARLES COLSON, *Loving God*[1]

Being sure of something we hope for and certain of something that we cannot see—this is the way of faith described in the Bible. In the Old Testament, the Jews had to live out such faith without knowledge of Jesus, personal access to God, or the testimony of the fulfillment of Scripture. As believers today, we have the written Scriptures, the New Testament witness, and the resurrection of Christ to offer us hope. We also have the Holy Spirit who enables us to understand, obey, and, when we fail, reassure us that we are forgiven.

But how effectively are we living our faith before our children? My husband recently wrote in a letter to some friends, "Often we are so busy teaching our children to obey and to follow the laws of Scripture that we fail to demonstrate what it really means to love Christ and walk by faith before Him."

Teaching by Faith

1. When God created the nation of Israel, He intended it to represent Himself to all the world. His people were to obey His commands and pass on His truths to their children. Read Deuteronomy 6:4-9, keeping in mind that in this passage the word *teach* means "to repeat."

   a. List all the ways parents are to demonstrate their relationship with God.

   b. How might you translate these activities into today's culture? How might you incorporate these activities into your lifestyle?

2. Now read Deuteronomy 6:10-19.

   a. What does God warn parents about concerning their own relationship with Him?

   b. If we ignored God's warning and did what He commands us not to do in this passage, how might our behavior affect our children?

3. In Deuteronomy 6:20-25, a child speaks. Read that passage.

   a. What question does the child ask?

   b. According to this passage, how should the parents answer the child?

c. Why was it important for parents to teach the child about their deliverance from Egypt?

d. What do these verses teach about why obedience is important for parents and children alike?

In Deuteronomy, God says, "These things should be *on your heart.*" (verse 6, emphasis added). If something is really on our heart, we can't help but talk about it with others. Does your child know what is on your heart? Have you shared with your child, as God tells parents here, that you were once a slave to another ruler? Do they know the story of God freeing you from that ruler and changing you into the person you are today? Have you shared with your children the miracles He has worked in your life to protect you, provide for you, and make you more like Jesus?

4. Think through the stories from Deuteronomy. (Remember that the word *teach* means "to repeat.")

a. What story of your spiritual journey can you tell your children in two different ways? (Different ways will keep the story exciting for them.)

b. If you are meeting with a group, share one story with your group.

If you haven't told your children the stories of God's personal work in your life, plan a time when you can begin to share these things in a casual, natural setting. Remember, you need to demonstrate that your relationship with God is ongoing and that He continues to teach us daily when we spend time with Him.

Our love for God must be complete. It is impossible for me to transfer to my child a principle I do not personally embrace, that is, a love for God that permeates all my heart. It is impossible for me to convince my child of the value of honesty, for example, if I am dishonest. Impossible for me to convey to my child the necessity of clean lips if I habitually practice profanity. It is impossible for children to grasp the importance of care and compassion for others if their parents run roughshod over others. Our love for God must be an all-encompassing love, a deep-down dedication. It will be on your heart, not simply a nice-sounding religious idea washing around in your mind.

CHARLES R. SWINDOLL, *Growing Wise in Family Life²*

A Mom's Memory

Several years ago we were trying to sell a car by advertising in the newspaper. After many days a man decided to buy it. As we were finalizing the paperwork to complete the transaction, the buyer casually said, "Of course you'll adjust the figures when you submit this so I don't have to pay tax, won't you?"

Knowing how much we needed to sell this car, our junior-high daughter listened carefully for her father's response, and she heard him say that he would make no adjustment that was not true. We all knew that the man could back out of the sale. His was the only response we had received from our advertising, and we desperately needed the money from the sale to help us with our upcoming move. Yet her father acted on biblical faith and obeyed without knowing the outcome

What was *on my husband's heart* came out in his behavior! In spite of our very real financial need, he represented Christ to all of us at that moment when he stood by the truth. How I praised God that He gave my daughter's father the strength to reflect His character and live by faith instead of fear. This lesson on honesty was more important than all of our Bible lessons on the subject.

5. a. When was one time when God helped you make a hard decision by faith?

   b. Plan a time when you can share this experience with your children. The story will be valuable no matter what the outcome of the event.

Planned Opportunities for Teaching

Often we realize ahead of time that God is giving us opportunities to teach our children about living a life of faith. One of those times came for my husband and me when we were asked to move to another state. Our daughter, then 11, hadn't moved since her birth. Although we knew the move would involve big adjustments for us all, we realized that God was giving her an opportunity to see Him work in her life in very personal ways. Because of the stability she had known for eleven years, she had no need to trust God for school, for friends, for her future. These had all been in place for her since the beginning of her life. With the family's move, she would have an opportunity to see God bring forth those things from nothing and to learn about His faithfulness to her. During our move she began to learn that God wants to do things in her life as well as her parents' lives.

In the book of Exodus, we read about opportunities the children of Israel, God's chosen people, had to trust Him and see Him work in their lives. The Hebrews had been enslaved by Egypt's new pharaoh, but despite their hard life, the people of Israel increased in number. Threatened by this growth, Pharaoh commanded the Hebrew midwives to kill all the male babies that were born. But the midwives honored God, let the boys live, and lied to Pharaoh to cover up their actions. Pharaoh then commanded all his people to throw every boy that was born to a Hebrew woman into the Nile River.

6. Read Exodus 2:1-10, the account of the birth of Moses, the man whom God chose to deliver His people from their long captivity. Write down your observations in the following categories.

a. Choices

What risk was involved in the choices this mother made?

What do her actions tell you about her faith?

How did the mother's choices involve her daughter?

What steps of faith did the daughter take as she obeyed her mother?

b. Results

What could have resulted from the mother's actions?

What could have resulted from the daughter's actions?

What lessons did mother and daughter learn when they stepped out in faith?

Jochebed, Moses' mother, made careful plans for saving her son, although she had no promise from God that her plans would work. Nevertheless, she stepped out in faith and even involved her daughter, not knowing what the outcome would be for the infant Moses or young Miriam. The writer of Hebrews honors Jochebed's choice to believe God with these words: "By faith Moses, when he was born, was hidden for three months by his parents, because they saw he was a beautiful child; and *they were not afraid of the king's edict*" (11:23, NASB, emphasis added).

Sometimes we are fearful of what will happen to us or to our children if we step out into the unknown. But Jochebed took that step, and her young daughter was encouraged in her own faith by her mother's willingness to trust God. Jochebed acted by faith, which was based on her knowledge of the character of the God she served. She trusted Him to take her actions and use them to accomplish His purpose for her family. Miriam's life was forever affected by her mother's decision to act in faith.

7. Have you, like Jochebed, been willing to make a decision concerning your child's future, even when you were not sure of the outcome? If so, what did you learn from taking that step of faith?

In the love letters from our children that I mentioned earlier, these words from one daughter greatly encouraged us. As she remembered a time of rebellion in her teenage years she said, "You committed my life to God. You knew that He would give me the strength to do the right thing." At the time, my daughter knew that I was struggling to trust her to God's care. God helped both of us through that time of trial, and we both learned a lot about faith through the experience. I learned that God could accomplish things in my daughter's life that were impossible for me to do. She learned that God could enable her to obey Him in the midst of great temptation if she would commit herself to His care.

Unplanned Opportunities to Teach

Jesus was the master at seizing unexpected opportunities for teaching His disciples. He often used interruptions in their schedule and encounters with people in need to train them in faith. Through it all, Jesus consistently modeled His dependence on the Father. And, although He rarely talked to His disciples about prayer, they recognized His dependence on His Father by His consistent prayer. Jesus' faith—His close relationship with God—was evident in all areas of His life as He walked through the ordinary events of each day. Likewise, we must demonstrate our faith in the dailiness of life, even if we don't always know what might result from our steps of faith. In fact, acting when the outcome isn't known is the greatest demonstration of all because it shows we trust God no matter what!

8. Our children must see us depend on the Lord Christ as we live by faith and walk daily with Him. Read the Lord's Prayer (below) and then record what Jesus prays regarding priorities, provision, relationships, and rewards.

"Our Father who art in heaven,
Hallowed be Thy name.
Thy kingdom come.
Thy will be done

On earth as it is in heaven.
Give us this day our daily bread.
And forgive us our debts,
    as we also have forgiven debtors.
And do not lead us into
    temptation, but deliver
    us from evil.
For Thine is the kingdom, and the power,
and the glory, forever. Amen."
(MATTHEW 6:9-13, NASB)

Priorities

Provision

Relationships

Rewards

9. Having considered Jesus' prayer in a general way, now look at what
   His words here can teach you about walking in faith.

   a. In which area of your life—priorities, provision, relationships,
      and rewards—do you need to depend more on the Lord? Please
      explain why you chose that area.

   b. What changes in your attitude or your actions must occur for you
      to begin walking by faith in this area of your life?

For Personal Meditation

10. Meditate on the following passage, especially its description of God.

Now to Him who is able to do exceeding abundantly beyond all that we ask or think, according to the power that works within us. (Ephesians 3:20, NASB)

a. What is one specific area of your life that seems beyond your ability to change?
b. What does God promise to do in this verse?

For Personal Prayer

As a mother in training, commit yourself to praying about that area of your life where you aren't wholeheartedly trusting God. Ask Him to help you walk by faith and record in your journal (as we practiced in chapter two) the desire of your heart to grow in faith in this area. Also, make yourself accountable to someone who will help you. Finally, ask God to remind you of His presence and His promised faithfulness when you find yourself facing an opportunity to walk by faith, not by sight.

TRAIN UP A MOM:
To Love Supernaturally

*Love is very patient and kind, never jealous or envious,
never boastful or proud, never haughty or selfish or rude.
Love does not demand its own way. It is not irritable or
touchy. It does not hold grudges and will hardly even notice
when others do it wrong. It is never glad about injustice, but
rejoices whenever truth wins out. If you love someone you
will be loyal to him no matter what the cost. You will always
believe in him, always expect the best of him, and always
stand your ground in defending him.*

1 CORINTHIANS 13:4-7, TLB

The fountains from which love flows are in God,
not in us. It is absurd to think that the love of God is
naturally in our hearts, as a result of our own nature. His love
is there only because it *has been poured out in our hearts by
the Holy Spirit. . . .* (Romans 5:5)

OSWALD CHAMBERS, *My Utmost for His Highest*[1]

When I became a believer, I was amazed to read these words in the Bible
one day: "Encourage the young women to love their husbands, to love
their children" (Titus 2:4, NASB). As a young mother I sometimes did not
like my children's behavior, but here I saw that I had to receive training
in how to love them. In fact, the older the children grew, the more I realized they had to be loved with a supernatural love. My natural love was
not enough. And not only did I have to love supernaturally, but I also had
to love individually. After all, every child is different. Then, when I read
God's definition of love in 1 Corinthians 13, I became even more convinced
that the kind of love my children needed from me was not natural.

Qualities of Supernatural Love

1. In His parable of the prodigal son, Jesus gives us a picture of the love God has for His children. Read Luke 15:11-32.

   a. Describe the younger son's behavior.

   b. Why might it have been difficult for his father to continue to love him?

   c. In verses 20-24, how does the father demonstrate his supernatural love for his younger son?

   d. Which of those qualities would have been most difficult for you?

There must be some circumstances during which love has to suffer a long time in order to be real love.

EDITH SCHAEFFER, *What Is a Family?*[2]

2. Look again at Luke 15:25-32.

   a. What words and actions reveal the elder son's attitude toward his brother's return? Describe the attitude he demonstrates.

b. Now describe the kind of relationship you think the elder son had with his father.

c. What about the elder brother would have made it difficult for you to love him if you had been his father?

d. What qualities of supernatural love were demonstrated by the Father toward the elder son?

CRL

The Lord appeared to him from afar, saying,
"I have loved you with an everlasting love;
Therefore I have drawn you with lovingkindness."
JEREMIAH 31:3, NASB

CRL

In the story of the prodigal son, the father had to love both of his sons with a supernatural love. With that kind of love, the youngest finally "came to his senses" (verse 17). We don't know if the older son ever embraced the love his father freely offered him. We do see, however, that both brothers took advantage of the father's love and, to some extent, used him for their own purposes.

The younger son wanted his father's gifts and what they could buy for him, but he did not at first want the life his father offered him. After he received what he wanted, he began to recognize the value of what his father offered. Knowing he deserved nothing because of his behavior, he turned to the grace his father had demonstrated toward his servants. The younger son learned that relationship was not dependent upon his works, but upon humbling himself before his accepting father.

The older son enjoyed all the benefits and rewards of living with his father but with an ungrateful heart. He thought relationship was based on his works, that they were rewards for his faithfulness, and so he believed he deserved better treatment than his brother.

Like the father in the parable, the Lord Jesus Christ was used and rejected by the very ones He came to love. As John 1:11 says, "He came to His own, and those who were His own did not receive Him" (NASB).

If we are to reflect God's love for our children even when they reject or use us, we ourselves must be on intimate terms with His love. We must lean on Him so He can enable us to continue to love those who reject us or use our love for their own purposes. He alone is the source of supernatural love.

Webster's definition of *supernatural* is "existing or occurring outside the normal experience or knowledge of man; not explainable by the known forces or laws of nature; specifically of, involving or attributed to God."[3] The kind of love the Father gives to us to give to others is definitely not natural. It can only be explained as coming from God Himself. It is His nature in us, not our own nature. He graciously empowers us by His precious Spirit to give love as He does.

Practicing Supernatural Love

3. a. From 1 Corinthians 13:4-8, circle the two phrases below that mean the most to you. Explain why.

Love never gives up.
Love cares more for others than for self.
Love doesn't want what it doesn't have.
Love doesn't strut.
Doesn't have a swelled head,
Doesn't force itself on others,
Isn't always "me first,"
Doesn't fly off the handle,
Doesn't keep score of the sins of others,
Doesn't revel when others grovel,
Takes pleasure in the flowering of truth,
Puts up with anything,
Trusts God always,
Always looks for the best,
Never looks back,
But keeps going to the end.
Love never dies.
(1 Corinthians 13:4-8, MSG)

b. Give a personal example of how God has loved you supernaturally even when you behaved wrongly. Perhaps you can
also share a time God helped you love your child in one of
these ways.

We often don't know how to express our love. Furthermore, our children interpret how we express love to them in different ways, according to their own needs. Have you ever heard the phrase, *if looks could
kill?* Our children know if we are loving them by the expressions on our
face, our rolling eyes, our frustrated sighs, and our yelling in response
to their actions. All these things—our words, our tone of voice, our
deeds—must reflect the character of Christ, not our feelings at the
moment. First John 3:18 says it this way: "Let us not love with word or
with tongue, but in deed and truth" (NASB).

4. To what extent is your speech consistent with the truth that God has
revealed about love in 1 Corinthians 13?

5. Do your actions, even when you're disciplining your children,
demonstrate God's love and acceptance? Give a specific example.

6. How do your attitudes reflect the phrase, "Doesn't keep score of the
sins of others?" How would you or do you demonstrate this as a reality in your life to your children?

A Mom's Memory

My teenage child had been in rebellion for a long time. Her desires seemed to be completely opposed to everything we tried to teach her. There had been many battles during her high school years as we tried to enforce godly standards in our home. After graduation she was on her own, and the same trend continued in her life.

I was very weary, close to giving up hope, and almost at the point of doubting God's faithfulness. I was filled with memories of failure; I was tired of trying to love this "unlovely child" and enduring her rejection. I had no more strength to give. One day as I vacuumed my bedroom, I was crying and praying to God, asking Him either to help me keep on in this struggle or to end her rebellion. I flung the vacuum aside and fell across the bed, pleading with God for relief from this trial. The words He brought to my heart did not feel very much like comfort:

For what credit is there if, when you sin and are harshly treated, you endure it with patience? But if when you do what is right and suffer for it you patiently endure it, this finds favor with God. (1 Peter 2:20, NASB)

Although this sounded more like a rebuke than comfort, God said exactly what I needed to hear. He was reminding me that He wanted to love my daughter through me. He was asking me to love this "unlovely child" in the same way He had loved me when I paid no attention to Him. To recognize that I was out of strength to love her was exactly what I needed to do in order to gain supernatural love through His Spirit. I confessed my lack of dependence on Him as well as my independent spirit, my thinking that I could love her in my own strength.

As I picked up my vacuum, my heart was filled with renewed strength and my mind was full of new ideas on how to love my unlovely child!

Recently I read with joy these words in a love letter to me from this formerly unlovely child: "You have become something I thought my mother would never be: *a close friend.* Our conversations and your prayers and opinions mean so much to me. They always set me back on track when I have a problem or need a listening ear." The unlovely child has become a testimony to God through her love and devotion to Him. When my natural love failed, my faithful God helped me to love my daughter supernaturally.

For Personal Meditation

7. As you think about supernatural love, meditate on the following verses:

For while we were still helpless, at the right time Christ died for the ungodly. For one will hardly die for a righteous man; though perhaps for the good man someone would dare even to die. But God demonstrates His own love toward us, in that while we were yet sinners, Christ died for us. (Romans 5:6-8, NASB)

a. Notice the word "helpless" in the passage. How were you helpless when you came to Christ?

b. How has God demonstrated His love to you personally? Be specific.

c. Which of your children seems to be the most helpless right now?

d. How is that child acting out that helplessness through his or her behavior?

e. How could you demonstrate your love to them in a new way?

For Personal Prayer

We need have no fear of someone who loves us perfectly; His perfect love for us eliminates all dread of what He might do to us. If we are afraid, it is for fear of what He might do to us, and shows that we are not fully convinced that He really loves us. (1 JOHN 4:18, TLB)

Tell God one way in which you feel you are failing in your attempt to love your child. Tell Him about your fears for your child. First Peter 5:7 says, "Cast all your anxiety on him because he cares for you." Give to God each anxious thought that He has brought to mind about your children. Ask Him for new ways to love them each individually. Pray for wisdom concerning how and when to implement the ideas God gives you.

TRAIN UP A MOM:
To Study Her Children

Train up a child in the way he should go,
(and in keeping with his individual gift or bent),
and when he is old he will not depart from it.
PROVERBS 22:6, AMP

There is no more influential or powerful role on earth
than a mother's. As significant as political, military,
educational, or religious figures may be, none can compare
to the impact made by mothers. Their words are never
fully forgotten, their touch leaves an indelible impression,
and the memory of their presence lasts a lifetime.
CHARLES R. SWINDOLL, *Growing Strong in Family Life*[1]

As a parent, you may think you know your child well; there may be no doubt in your mind as to "the way he should go." After all, we want to train our children to follow God and lead productive lives in His service. But in Proverbs 22:6 from the Amplified Version, we see that training requires sensitivity to each child. We are to train our children *according to their individual gift or bent.*

The phrase translated "train up" has two meanings. The first refers to placing a rope around a horse's mouth to give it direction as it is being broken. The second meaning has to do with a preserve or jelly that a midwife placed in an infant's mouth right after birth. Rubbing the baby's mouth and gums with her finger created a desire to suck and made the baby thirsty. These word pictures suggest two types of training. In the first, someone imposes his will on another to bring that person into submission. The second involves creating a desire for something. These types of training are completely different, but both are necessary. As mothers in training, we eagerly desire our children to become thirsty for God through our example, but we also recognize that a necessary part of training children involves helping them choose wisely. Proverbs 29:15 says it this way:

The rod and reproof give wisdom,
But a child who gets his own way
brings shame to his mother. (NASB)

Perhaps you have already seen that what works for one of your children doesn't work for another. This should be no surprise since each child is unique, designed by God. Perhaps you have also realized that you respond differently to your children, that you seem to relate more easily to one than another. You probably get along better with the one who is most like you. Clearly, your children cannot be treated alike because their *bents* are different.

In the next two chapters we will explore several ways to study your children, to learn how God has bent them. I studied my children to find out their unique personalities, their personal values, their gifts and talents, and the things that cause them to stumble. I asked God to give me ideas on how to encourage their strengths and recognize their temptations. I'll be sharing methods I have used as well as the Scriptures I have studied as God has trained me.

Discovering Personality Tendencies

There are many different types of personalities presented in the Bible. This variety can give us insight into our children's bents. Generally we are a composite of several personalities, but we usually have strong tendencies in one direction. One way I have studied my children's personalities is to select word pictures as presented in the Song of Songs, from the Old Testament. Word pictures are also found in the parables, as Jesus often contrasted two people to illustrate a truth. *A word picture is a way of using words to create a picture in the mind of the reader.*

The following picture from the Song of Songs suggests two brothers discussing their younger sister's personality as she approaches adolescence. Look for the word picture suggested in these verses:

We have a young sister,
  and her breasts are not yet grown.
What shall we do for our sister
  for the day she is spoken for?

If she is a *wall*,
we will build towers of silver on her.
If she is a *door*,
we will enclose her with panels of cedar.
(Song of Songs 8:8-9, emphasis added)

1. What pictures come to your mind when you think of a wall? How could this apply to a person?

2. A door suggests different pictures. What tendencies could this personality have?

To me, the word picture of a wall represents a person who tends to be less open to other influences, to be able to stand on his or her own. The door suggests the opposite, someone who tends to be more susceptible to influences from others and less likely to have strong convictions. These are *tendencies*—most of us are combinations of wall and door.

As we grow and develop, we learn how to order our lives to function in this world, and we change our behavior accordingly. Then, upon entering a relationship with Christ and responding in obedience to His Word, the Holy Spirit begins to mold us into the perfect image of Jesus Christ. In a similar way, if we are training a child with the help of the Holy Spirit, and our child responds obediently, the Holy Spirit is also able to mold our child.

Still, as human beings uniquely created, we possess unique personalities. We demonstrate these by our conduct in life and by what is important to us: our values. Some children reveal their personalities quite early in their life, as the following passage demonstrates.

Two Different Personalities

After praying for many years for a child, Rebekah became pregnant with twin boys. Esau was born first, and Jacob quickly followed, holding tightly to Esau's heel. Although children of the same parents, Esau and Jacob were entirely different personalities. Read Genesis 25:24-34.

3. Beside each characteristic listed below, write the name of the son, Esau or Jacob, who best fits that description. (Some words will fit both sons.)

tolerant

self-indulgent

determined

athletic

good-natured

orderly

selfish

spontaneous

self-centered

quiet

controlling

rough

4. a. From your observations above, how would you describe Jacob's personality? (Include both his strengths and his weaknesses.)

b. How would you describe Esau's personality, both strengths and weaknesses?

5. In what ways are your children most like Jacob?

Child #1

Child #2

Child #3

In what ways do your children fit into Esau's personality?

Child #1

Child #2

Child #3

In addition to personality traits, God seems to assign each child a life situation, a collection of factors over which neither we nor our children have control. These include birth order, the financial resources of the parents, physical appearance, and so on.

6. Look back again at Genesis 25:24-34 to determine what these included for Esau.

a. What conditions of his life were handed to him that he could not control? Be specific.

b. Make the same observations about Jacob.

7. Think about each of your children. What are the unchangeable factors that God has allowed in their lives? (Consider your maturity at the time they were born, your resources, your background and experience to train them, etc.)

Child #1

Child #2

Child #3

8. Have you ever thanked God for the specific situation He placed them in? As you think about the situations God gave your children, are you more inclined to be grateful or resentful? Why?

God has placed you and your children exactly where you need to be; He has chosen the setting of your lives and that of your children as well. (At this point you may want to return to chapter three and review the passages from Psalm 139.) When you compare yourself with others, or your children with one another, you begin to doubt God's plan and can become jealous or discontent with His choices for you and your children. Instead, it is more helpful simply to take these unchangeable factors into account as we study our children.

A friend of mine clearly saw the different bents and personalities of her children when her family went to the beach on vacation. She found it interesting to see how her two children approached the ocean. One child ran as fast as he could and dived right in. The other child ran about halfway to the water and stopped. What a vivid picture of two different approaches to life, two different personality bents!

It is by his deeds that a lad distinguishes himself
If his conduct is pure and right.

The hearing ear and the seeing eye,
The LORD has made both of them.
(PROVERBS 20:11-12, NASB)

Discovering Potential Temptations

9. Think about each of your children. Mark where each one would fit on the scale below.

1	2	3	4	5	6	7	8	9	10

Like Esau focuses on short-term goals. Like a door, easily influenced

Like Jacob focuses on long-term goals Like a wall, not easily influenced

1	2	3	4	5	6	7	8	9	10

seeks personal pleasure

seeks personal security

1	2	3	4	5	6	7	8	9	10

can look "bad" to others

often appears "good" to others

10. a. If you have identified one of your children as being the most like Esau, what are the main challenges you might face in training that one?

b. What choices can you make to help that child consider future consequences of his or her behavior?

c. Look beyond this child's "bad" or inappropriate behavior. What stands out as desirable qualities in this child? Be specific and praise him or her for these.

d. What steps can you take to help this child avoid the tendency toward impulsive behavior?

11. a. If you have a Jacob, the child who looks "good" to others, what are the specific areas that might need to be addressed in his or her life?

b. When a child focuses on long-term goals, losing sight of people and their needs, he or she can appear selfish. What steps can you take to help your child in this area?

c. The elder brother we studied in chapter 5, from Luke 15:11-32, had the same tendencies toward temptation that Jacob did. What were that elder brother's temptations?

d. What specific steps can you take to help this kind of child learn to be loving to others and avoid making judgments about them?

12. Think about your own bent. Mark things in the following list that best describe your areas of temptations.

☐ losing my temper
☐ holding a grudge
☐ making rash decisions
☐ wanting to look good to others
☐ lack of self-control
☐ afraid of failure
☐ wanting control
☐ lack of compassion
☐ controlled by appetite
☐ other (please list more)

13. a. Which of your children is more like you?

b. Can you think of any ways you might be favoring him or her above your other children?

c. What specific steps can you take to enrich your relationship with the child who is not as much like you?

A Mom's Memory

When my children were in elementary school, one wrote a paper called, "I Can Handle It." In this story, which received an A+, she told of a baby in a crib who manipulated those around it to get what it wanted. At a young age my daughter was already concerned with getting her immediate needs met and using her skills to do it.

The other child wrote about who she wanted to be when she grew up. Her words clearly reflected her particular bent: "If I could be anybody in the world, I would like to be myself. I would not ever, never want to be anybody else. I am glad for who I am, I do not want to be anybody else." This daughter was confident that she was in the best place and that she would be able to have a good and successful life.

The first child was never tempted the way the second child was. Things were not that important to her. She was adept at figuring out how to get her way and didn't let people or rules interfere. People's opinions were not as important as personal freedom. She was, like Esau, easily influenced and out for pleasure. Today, as an adult walking with Christ, she has learned that rules are there for her good, and because of the love God has demonstrated to her in spite of her rebellion, she is able to give grace in a marvelous way to others.

Despite her confident essay, as the second child grew, she was tempted by the desire for approval, craved beautiful clothes, and needed to prove to others that she was worthy. She always wanted to look and act right in everything, just as Jacob did. Today, as a mother walking with Christ, she is learning to accept God's love for her without depending on her performance. She is putting people ahead of her personal goals, and learning to walk by faith and give grace to others.

Romans 3:23 says, "For all have sinned and fall short of the glory of God." We are all sinners, no matter how our personality tendencies or temptations appear to others. We are all in need of help from God to become who He created us to be. We can look very different to other people—often the "good," respectable person receives approval, while the "bad" person receives judgment—but God looks on the heart, while we look on the outside. The Pharisees were careful to look good on the outside and obey all the rules, but Jesus rebuked them for their coldness of heart and their dependence on their own efforts. The prodigal, "bad" son broke all the rules by looking elsewhere for satisfaction, rejecting the love his father offered him from his birth. But his father freely forgave his rebellion when he returned home, acknowledging his sin.

For Personal Meditation

14. Think about your children as you meditate on the following promise.

If any of you lacks wisdom, he should ask God, who gives generously to all without finding fault, and it will be given to him. (James 1:5)

15. a. Which child forces you to call on the wisdom of God most frequently?

b. What does God promise to do for you when you ask Him?

c. Write down one specific way God has helped you in this.

For Personal Prayer

Ask God to give you one new insight into each child's personality bent. Pray for that child in that area. Ask God to give you courage to help your children recognize and deal with their temptations.

Seven

TRAIN UP A MOM:
To Affirm Their Natural Bent

⌘

The LORD will accomplish
what concerns me;
Thy lovingkindness, O
LORD, is everlasting;
Do not forsake the works
of Thy hands.
PSALM 138:8, NASB

Then the potter said, "Sit down, and you can make a pot."
"That I cannot do, as you see what I have tried," I replied. "Sit
down," he insisted. I did so. Then, sitting behind me, he put
his arms over my arms, his hands over mine, his fingers over
my fingers. The wheel began to spin. "Do not allow your
fingers to resist mine," he advised, and I obeyed. There
under my fingers, to my astonishment grew a beautiful
vessel. The wheel stopped and my friend said, "Behold your
pot." "Not mine," I said. But the potter said, "Look on your
hands, there is clay on your fingers, so they touched the clay,
for there is nothing on my hand. Whose hand touches the
vessel, that hand makes the pot."
ANONYMOUS[1]

"Do not allow your fingers to resist mine." This quotation is the guide
for us as we train our children. God has given parents hands-on
opportunities with their children. It may be our arms and hands and fingers that touch their lives each day, but our dependence must be on the
One who is standing behind and directing us as we allow Him to. We
must respond to His leading personally and not resist His purpose and
plan as we train our children.

This section will include two more ways of studying our children: discovering our children's values and studying biblical characters. These methods are intended to confirm from another perspective things learned in chapter six.

Discovering Our Children's Values

Values are that quality of a thing according to which it is thought of as being more or less desirable, useful, estimable, important, etc. Values declare the degree of something's worth. In addition to studying our children's personality and temptations, we need to know what they value in life. As parents who love Christ, we desire to help our children value what the Scriptures teach is right in God's sight. But we must know how God has bent them in order to pray and point them toward positive values fitting their personalities.

1. As a teenager, Daniel was captured by the Babylonians when they invaded Jerusalem. He and several other young men were chosen to serve in Nebuchadnezzar's court and taught the language and literature of the Babylonians. Read Daniel 1:1-5.

   a. How are these young men described?

   b. What was to be their future?

   c. In verses 8-17, what choices did Daniel make about his lifestyle as a captive?

   d. What would you say Daniel valued? What was important to him?

2. Daniel and his friends continued to distinguish themselves in the king's court, but King Nebuchadnezzar allowed his pride to be used to test their loyalty to him.

a. Read Daniel 3:8-30. What choices did Daniel's friends make?

b. How did those choices reflect their values (what was important to them)?

c. How did God honor those values?

3. Does one of your children seem to be like Daniel and his friends, willing to stand up for what he knows is right even in the face of opposition? If so, which one?

Strong convictions are often a positive trait, as they were with Daniel and his friends. However, sometimes our greatest strengths are also our greatest weaknesses. For example, sometimes a child's strong convictions conflict with God's value system. In that case, we need to retrain those convictions, and that training is not always easy.

4. If you have a Daniel child, are there specific areas in which his strong convictions might need to be retrained to conform to God's value system? If so, what are those areas? Be as specific as you can.

5. a. As a parent, are you like Daniel in any ways? How does your behavior demonstrate your value system?

b. What areas in your life, in which you have strong convictions, might need to be brought under the guidance of the Scriptures?

Although taken captive as a boy, Daniel had a value system already established in his life. He had a strong desire to honor his God and to obey His laws in the midst of a foreign, oppressive culture. He stood up to the establishment and demonstrated his value system, the things of importance to him. A child like Daniel is most unusual; his strengths enable him to do extraordinary things when they are under the control of the Holy Spirit, as Daniel's seem to have been. However, if those values are not under God's control, it is very hard to convince such children that they could be wrong about anything. Like Jacob, they will move forward toward their goals, often without aligning them with God's goals for their lives. Like the Pharisees, they may need to be taught that God has a better plan for them than their own.

A Mom's Memory

One of our children, who is quite like Jacob and Daniel, demonstrated the value system she embraced even as a young child. From the start, she had her own way of doing things; she was even specific about bedtime rituals. She had definite opinions about most things. However, she found it hard to admit she could be wrong about anything.

When she turned 16, she applied for a driver's license. I knew she could drive, but in her confidence she had not studied adequately for the test. Knowing her need to depend on God and be faithful to study, I actually prayed she would fail the test. I knew my child needed to have her values, her confidence, shaped by God. God was faithful, and she did fail the test. We spent the next day crying together and talking about this need in her life. It was actually more difficult for her to admit she had been wrong and acknowledge her failure than to have to repeat the test. Recently, this young woman had her value system challenged again as she studied the Scriptures, realizing that she had erroneously interpreted a certain passage. True to her nature and value system, she was quick to respond to what God was saying to her. She was willing to change when she understood clearly that her interpretation was incorrect. God again reshaped her strong convictions to conform to His truth.

Samson's parents received news of his coming birth through a visit from an angel, who gave specific instructions concerning how he was to be trained. His parents raised him according to the Jewish law and the angel's orders. Like Daniel, Samson's family was also in bondage; this time the Philistines had conquered Israel. But he was in his own country and home, and therefore was allowed to follow Jewish traditions.

6. a. Read Judges 13:1-5. Describe how Samson's parents were raising this promised child and why they were to be so careful in what they allowed in his life.

   b. What conclusions can you draw from Judges 14:1-10 about what Samson thought was important for his life?

   c. Read Judges 16:4-7,15-20. What values that would illustrate God to others did Samson violate in this passage?

   d. During his captivity at the hands of the Philistines, Samson prayed to God to restore his strength so he could have revenge on his enemies. Read Judges 16:25-30. How did this desire fit into God's value system (see the promise in Judges 13:5)?

7. Do you have a child that seems, like Samson, to choose values that will eventually cause harm to himself or others? What are those values?

8. a. As a parent, can you identify any way in which you choose to disregard the values God has set before you? If so, what are they?

   b. What specific steps will you take to obey God?

Although Samson had great potential to be used of God, he tended to reject God's values and go his own way. In spite of this tendency for self-satisfaction, God used his life. He was a leader in Israel for twenty years, and he did "begin the deliverance of Israel from the hands of the Philistines" (Judges 13:5) as promised, although certainly not in the way his parents would have wanted. While seeking revenge on the Philistines, he destroyed himself along with the rulers and all the people in the temple.

When we or our children reject God's values and interpret them according to our desires, we cause suffering for others or suffer ourselves. One way to build God's values into a child's life is to do as this passage suggests:

> How can a young man keep his way pure?
> By living according to your word.
> I seek you with all my heart;
>   do not let me stray from your commands.
> I have hidden your word in my heart
>   that I may not sin against you.
> (PSALM 119:9-11)

9. What choices can you make as a parent to begin to build the Word of God into your own life? What choices will you make for your children?

Daniel and Samson illustrate different personalities, different temptations, and different value systems. Both of them were probably trained in godly living at a young age, but the expression of that training looked quite different as they grew. Because of his strong values and commitment, Daniel was able to stand up for God in a hostile environment. Later in life, Daniel demonstrated that his values were based on his hope in God when he was thrown into a lion's den because he prayed faithfully to the Hebrew God. Samson, although in a safer situation, still made choices that answered his short-term needs, as had Esau. He continued to fall into sinful situations because he did not seem to have the strong personal conviction needed to make right choices.

God planned our children exactly for us. The Daniels are no better than the Samsons to Him; He loves them both. As parents, we must look to God to show us how to help and guide them.

O our God, wilt Thou not judge them? For we are powerless
before this great multitude who are coming against us; nor do
we know what to do, but our eyes are on Thee.
2 CHRONICLES 20:12, NASB

Discovering Biblical Characters

Studying characters in the Bible has helped me learn about training my children. As I see how God worked in the life of a person, I study to learn how I might resemble him or her through my personality, my temptations, or my value system. Then I do the same kind of study for my children to learn from the example set by biblical characters. You've seen how much you can learn about your children by comparing them to Jacob and Esau, the two sons in Luke 15, Daniel, or Samson. I'd like to close this section by showing how studying one more biblical character's strengths and weaknesses can help us understand both our children and ourselves.

When I do a character study, I first find all the passages about the person I want to study. (You can find them in a concordance.) Then I ask myself questions to help me learn about the person.

For instance, study these passages about King David to learn from his example with his children.

10. Read 2 Samuel 11. What does this story reveal about David's character, temptations, and values? Note the positive and negative behavior patterns David followed.

11. a. Read 2 Samuel 12. What were David's strengths? How does this passage demonstrate them? What encouraging patterns do you see in his life?

b. What were David's weaknesses? How does this passage reveal them?

12. Now look at 2 Samuel 13 and consider David's example as a parent.

a. List the ways David's children failed to follow God's best for their lives.

b. How did David handle his family problems?

c. Why do you think David didn't punish Amnon? How do you think David's own weakness in the sexual area might have influenced his dealings with Amnon?

d. As David remembered his murder of Uriah, Bathsheba's husband, how do you think these memories affected him when his son Absalom murdered Amnon?

As his many psalms demonstrate, David had a deep relationship with God. However, he also struggled with many human failings. To watch his growth, we have only to read the psalms to see how he cried out to God for mercy and grace. As we study characters in Scripture, we often like to see positive role models emerging, preferring to choose someone we resemble in a positive way. But the purpose of our study is that we might profit from the mistakes of biblical characters as well, recognizing our tendency to make the same wrong choices or choose God's best in a similar circumstance. The examples we discover of success or failure can help us learn things about ourselves and our children when we are in similar circumstances. As you study a particular character, ask God to teach you how that study can profit you in the training of your child.

Another goal of studying biblical characters is to learn how to place your hope in God. If we put our hope in our own efforts or our children's successes, we will be disappointed. But when we place our hope in God and His faithfulness, we will not be disappointed. We have His promise that He will be with us even when we have trials. He will never leave us.

❧

"Never will I leave you;
never will I forsake you."
HEBREWS 13:5

❧

For Personal Meditation

13. Read the following verse.

> Blessed is he whose help is the God of Jacob,
>   whose hope is in the LORD his God,
> the Maker of heaven and earth,
>   the sea, and everything in them—
>   the LORD, who remains faithful forever.
> (Psalm 146:5-6)

a. List some things or people in which you have wrongly placed your hope.

b. What does this verse say about God's ability to help you with your hope? What specific areas do you need to surrender to Him concerning your hopes?

For Personal Prayer

Ask God for direction with your personal battles as you bring your life before Him. Thank Him for His faithful promise to help you as you hope in Him. Trust Him with each child individually.

TRAIN UP A MOM:
To Claim God's Promises

ॐ

For the promise is for you and your children,
and for all who are far off, as many as the Lord
our God shall call to Himself.
ACTS 2:39, NASB

When God wants a great work done in the world, or a great
wrong righted, He goes about it in a very unusual way. He
doesn't stir up His earthquakes, or send forth His
thunderbolts. Instead, He has a helpless baby born, perhaps
in a simple home and of some obscure mother. And then
God puts the idea into the mother's heart, and she puts it
into the baby's mind. And then God waits. The greatest
forces in the world are not the earthquakes and the
thunderbolts; the greatest forces in the world are babies!
RAY C. STEDMAN, *Guidelines for the Home Series*[1]

When I first began to study the Word of God, I eagerly looked for assurances that my children would follow the path of righteousness. I read all I could find about ways to make sure that I did things *right* in raising them. The one verse that I really held fast was Proverbs 22:6: "Train up a child in the way he should go, even when he is old he will not depart from it (NASB)." I considered this a *promise* from God.

Even as I claimed this verse, I struggled with contradictions that I observed in life and experience and in exceptions in Scripture. It seemed as though plenty of godly parents ended up with rebellious adult children. What was wrong?

Webster's Dictionary defines a *promise* as "an oral or written agreement to do or not to do something." The verb to promise means "to give a basis for expectation."[2] In contrast, a *principle* is "a fundamental truth, law, doctrine, or motivating force upon which others are based; a natural or original tendency, faculty, or endowment."[3]

Principles and promises are very important, but we should keep the two distinct in our minds. The book of Proverbs, for instance, is a book of *principles*. It outlines the best way for those who know God to live, and it contains guidelines for those who don't know Him personally. Proverbs teaches us the good and the bad about people, and shows us the consequences of their choices in life. Solomon, the writer of many proverbs, knew these principles but failed to follow them in his own life. He was very successful in the world's eyes, but he failed to obey God. Earthly success may come from following Proverbs' principles, but living according to the principles will not ensure a relationship with Christ.

Vine's Expository Dictionary of Biblical Words explains a promise this way: "It frequently stands for the thing promised by God, and so signifies a gift graciously bestowed, *not* a pledge secured by negotiation."[4]

We cannot negotiate with God as we do with one another. He has already graciously offered us a relationship with Jesus Christ, which we do not deserve. When God gives us a promise, it is usually not based on what we do, but rather what He does as a gift to us. We receive what is promised not because we follow all the principles, but because God is a gracious God who "demonstrates His own love toward us, in that while we were yet sinners, Christ died for us" (Romans 5:8, NASB).

The *principle* in Proverbs 22:6 was true. I realized I needed to study my children so that I could understand how God had designed them for His glory and ask for His help to train them accordingly. But recognizing my inability to follow all the guidelines was discouraging, until I remembered that the promise of God gives us something we can't accomplish on our own. I should not base my trust on my ability to follow the principles perfectly; no one ever could. Nor should I assume that if my children turned out well, it was due to my ability to train them. Rather, the promises we base our lives upon are given undeservedly by God's grace, and we are asked to trust Him for the results.

So, a *principle* is a general rule to guide our choices and a *promise* is an assurance from God that we are asked to trust and believe.

In this lesson we will study promises God gave to two sets of biblical parents. We'll learn from these examples why it's important to look for, rely upon, and pray about promises God gives us about our children.

Discovering Personal Promises

While the Jews were under Roman occupation, they were still allowed to practice their religious traditions. Jewish priests offered animal sacrifices several times a day in the temple at Jerusalem. They also entered the Holy Place of the temple twice a day to burn incense, a symbol of the nation's prayers being offered up to God. Any male descended from Aaron was automatically a priest. They were organized in divisions, and a man served when his turn came. The priests drew lots for the special jobs like offering the incense, and because there were many priests, a man might win this honor only a few times in his life.

One day a priest named Zechariah drew the job of offering the incense. Luke describes Zechariah and his wife, Elizabeth, as "upright in the sight of God, observing all the Lord's commandments and regulations blamelessly. But they had no children, because Elizabeth was barren; and they were both well along in years" (Luke 1:6-7).

When Zechariah entered the Holy Place to offer the incense and prayers, an angel from the Lord appeared to him. The angel's message was an answer to Israel's prayers as well as to the more personal prayers of Zechariah and Elizabeth for a child. The people of Israel had long prayed for a deliverer, for the Messiah promised long ago through the prophets. This angel reported that God was sending a messenger who would announce the Messiah's coming, and that messenger would be the long-awaited, long-prayed-for child of Zechariah and Elizabeth.

1. a. Read Luke 1:5-17. How did the angel describe this promised child?

b. What was to be the child's purpose?

c. How did Zechariah respond to this promise from God? (See verse 18.)

d. What do you think God was trying to teach Zechariah?

2. Read Luke 1:57-66 and explain how God fulfilled His promise.

We don't know how long Zechariah and Elizabeth lived after the birth of John, so we don't know if they lived to see how God's promise was fulfilled in John's life. Look up the following Scripture to see how God's purpose was served by this long-prayed-for child.

3. The gospel of Matthew tells us about John's ministry. By birth John was a priest, but rather than following the traditional ministry of his father, John chose to model his life after the Old Testament prophet Elijah. From Matthew 3:1-8, describe John's lifestyle and manner of ministry.

Since the Jews were under Roman occupation, they were required to pay taxes to the Romans. Often the tax collectors were Jews, despised by their fellow citizens as traitors. Roman soldiers were also employed to ensure obedience to the Roman law. These unpopular people, along with much of the Jewish populace, traveled to the desert to hear this new prophet, John.

4. a. Read Luke 3:1-20. List the types of people who came to hear John. What was his message to each type of person?

   b. Who is the last person mentioned in Luke's account, and what was the result of John's message to him?

King Herod put John in prison because John had publicly rebuked Herod for marrying his brother's ex-wife. While in prison, John began to doubt that Jesus was really the Messiah. John did not understand Jesus's ministry; like most other Jews, John expected Jesus to overthrow the Romans and become king. So John sent some of his disciples to inquire of Jesus and answer his doubts. Jesus reassured John's disciples and then turned to the crowd to discuss John.

5. Read Matthew 11:1-19. How did Jesus describe John to the people?

6. a. God's plan for John allowed King Herod's devastating intervention. Read Matthew 14:1-13. How did John's ministry end?

   b. What was Jesus' response to John's death?

Zechariah and Elizabeth were respected in the community, but their son probably looked more like a *hippie* than the son of a priest. His views were not popular with the religious people, his ministry was not traditional like his father's, and his life was cut short by an evil king. Nevertheless, John did fulfill his purpose as originally stated by the angel. John was the messenger in Luke 1:17 about whom it was declared, "and it is he who will go as a forerunner before Him" (NASB). God allowed John to fulfill God's purpose before he was killed, and at just the right time for Jesus to begin His ministry.

When we claim God's promises, we must give God freedom to interpret them in His time, and in His way.

7. If you had been Zechariah or Elizabeth, how do you think you would have responded to the way God fulfilled His promise concerning your son?

8. a. Has God ever answered your prayers for someone in a different way than you anticipated? If so, how did you respond to that answer?

   b. If you did not understand the answer at that time, how has your understanding changed over time?

The Lord is not slow in keeping His promise, as some under-
stand slowness. He is patient with you, not wanting anyone to
perish, but everyone to come to repentance.
2 PETER 3:9

Had I been Joseph's mother I'd have prayed protection from his
brothers: God keep him safe; he is so young, so different from
the others. Mercifully she never knew there would be slavery
and prison, too.

Had I been Moses' mother I'd have wept to keep my little
son; praying she might forget the babe drawn from the water of
the Nile, have I not kept him for her nursing him the while? Was
he not mine and she but Pharaoh's daughter?

Had I been Daniel's mother I should have pled, Give victory!
This Babylonian horde . . . godless and cruel . . . don't let them
take him captive . . . better dead, Almighty Lord!

Had I been Mary . . . Oh, had I been she, I would have
cried, Anything, O God, anything . . . but crucified!

With such prayers importunate my finite wisdom would
assail Infinite Wisdom; God, how fortunate Infinite Wisdom
should prevail!

RUTH BELL GRAHAM, *Sitting by My Laughing Fireplace*[5]

How God Gives Promises

As Ruth Bell Graham's poem reflects, our wisdom is not enough when
it comes to knowing which promises to claim for our children or how
to pray for them. Still, we shouldn't stop doing either one. As I mentioned in lesson 2, I use my personal time with the Lord to learn how
and what to pray for my children. When I consistently spend time with
God and ask Him to help me use the different study methods for each
child, I am often directed toward a particular verse to pray for them. It
is not a question of demanding a promise from God or searching for one
to the exclusion of worshiping Him. Instead, all of the promises have
come in the course of my daily time with Him, usually as I write in my
journal concerning His plan for my day. All of the promises have been
burned into my heart, a secret between God and me that I shared with

no one for a while. But each time I prayed for my child, that particular verse would come to my mind and spirit, demonstrating it was from His heart to mine.

A Mom's Memory

One of our children shared the characteristics of Esau and Samson; she tended to be like a door. I knew this from the time she was quite young. One morning as I spent my daily time with God, I was impressed by a particular verse in Isaiah 49:25. I was not searching for a promise at all, just reading my scheduled place in the Bible. This verse said, "Surely, thus says the LORD, 'Even the captives of the mighty man will be taken away, and the prey of the tyrant will be rescued; For I will contend with the one who contends with you, and I will save your sons'" (NASB). This verse had my daughter's name written all over it. Although there was no evidence of trouble or rebellion in her life at that time, whenever I prayed for her this verse came to mind. I wrote it in my journal on her special page, and recorded the date I received it. Later, however, when the storms of her life did arrive, I held tightly to this promise from God for her.

For many years I believed it by faith because I felt I was losing the battle for this child. Then God gave me another promise for her: "He put a new song in my mouth; a song of praise to our God; many will see and fear, and will trust in the LORD" (Psalm 40:3, NASB). I have seen God fulfill these promises in my daughter's life in a way that I could never have imagined. He has put the new song in her mouth, and in mine, and those who have prayed for her over the years have learned to trust the Lord in a new way. He is still working in her life, and still training me to trust Him for my children.

In Genesis 12:2, God promised Abraham that he would become a great nation. At the time, Abraham was 75 years old, and he and his wife, Sarah, had no children. As they tried to believe this promise for a number of years, they discovered just how much they needed to learn about their own faith.

9. a. How did God encourage Abraham and Sarah in each of the following passages?

Genesis 15:1-6

Genesis 17:1-6

Genesis 18:1-10

Genesis 21:1-8

b. How did Abraham and Sarah try to accomplish God's purpose through their own efforts in Genesis 16:1-6?

c. Twenty-five years elapsed between God's first promise to Abraham and the actual birth of Isaac. How do you respond when, after praying for a long time, nothing seems to happen?

10. a. According to Genesis 18:9-15, what was Sarah's attitude toward God's promise?

b. What did God say to Abraham about Sarah's attitude?

c. Why do you think Sarah had this attitude about God's promise?

11. What impossible things was God asking Sarah and Abraham to believe as He trained them to persevere in His promise?

12. Have you ever had a sense that God was saying something personally to you about your life or your child's? If so, what was it?

Perhaps, like Abraham and Sarah, you have had difficulty believing God after waiting many years for a particular promise to be fulfilled. When we read about them in Hebrews 11, God's view of them is very positive. Their struggles of faith are not recorded there but in Genesis. Failing to trust and obey was part of their training. These heroes of faith had to, as we do, look by faith to what was not visible to them at the moment and wait for God to fulfill His promise. A *promise* remember, is something that God does that we cannot do; it is a gift of His grace.

*For no matter how many promises God has made, they are
"Yes" in Christ. And so through him the "Amen" is spoken by us
to the glory of God.*
2 CORINTHIANS 1:20

For Personal Meditation

13. Look at the following verse. Underline the things God wants to do for you. Circle the things you must do to enjoy the fruits of this promise.

"For I know the plans that I have for you," declares the LORD, "plans for welfare and not for calamity to give you a future and a hope. Then you will call upon Me and come and pray to Me, and I will listen to you. And you will seek Me and find Me, when you search for me with all your heart." (Jeremiah 29:11-13, NASB)

14. What promises are you asking God to fulfill in your personal life?

15. How has God encouraged you through this chapter to believe His promises?

For Personal Prayer

God is a promise maker and a promise keeper. Ask God to give you the grace to call on Him, to come to Him, and pray with all your heart. Ask Him to lead you to those promises He has for each of your children.

TRAIN UP A MOM:
To Pray and Plan

I will instruct you and teach you in the way you should go;
I will counsel you and watch over you.
Do not be like the horse or the mule,
which have no understanding
but must be controlled by bit and bridle
or they will not come to you.
Many are the woes of the wicked,
but the LORD's unfailing love
surrounds the man who trusts in Him.
PSALM 32:8-10

Time spent in prayer and planning
helps us see our children as God does.
Prayer and planning aligns us with His purposes for them.
JEAN FLEMING, *A Mother's Heart* [1]

Walls and doors, discovering personality types, temptations, and values, learning how to claim promises for our children—does all this sound like *work?* Well, it is work. If we take seriously the job of raising our children, it will involve thinking, planning, and prayer, and all of these take time and effort. We want to be found faithful in our responsibility as parents. To do that, we must know, among other things, how to give, what to give, and when to give our children the things they need at the proper time. This involves much more than physical needs; it also involves decisions regarding their mental, emotional, and spiritual well-being every single day.

In this chapter, you will begin to make a special page in your journal for each of your children. You will continue to have specific direction as to how to pray and plan to help them grow.

Discovering Needs

How well do you know your child? Answer the following questions for each of your children. Don't ask them the questions, just answer as well as you can to test how well you really know your children. Set aside a page in your journal for each child, and write your answers there.

1. a. Who is your child's hero?

   b. What is your child's biggest fear?

   c. What makes your child angry?

   d. Of what accomplishment is your child most proud?

   e. What has been your child's biggest disappointment?

   f. What makes your child feel happy?

   g. What do you do that makes him or her feel sad?

Just as you have different answers for each child, you'll have to make the appropriate applications for each one also.

☙

I believe strongly that Proverbs 22:6 is a command to train the whole person . . . intellectually, spiritually, culturally, emotionally . . . in things of creativity, in understanding the whole of history, in relationships with people, and in seeing something of the tremendous scope of the universe from the viewpoint that God exists, God is the Creator, and that He has made us with the capacities we have in His image, to think and act and feel and create on a finite level.

EDITH SCHAEFFER, *What is a Family?*[2]

☙

2. Read Luke 2:52. Under each heading in the chart below describe how Jesus grew.

Physical	Mental	Spiritual	Social

3. a. Think about each of your children, and put each one's name under the areas above in which he or she needs more attention.

   b. Just under the child's name, write a specific way that you might help him or her mature in this area.

   c. Keep a current list, and ask God to give you creative ideas and thoughts for each one.

The specific needs of each child will call for different and specific plans. In the physical realm, taking my daughter to the playground helped build both physical and social needs in her life. Helping your child mentally could mean spending special time each day on a subject he or she is struggling with, or perhaps finding a tutor for him or her. Encouraging your children spiritually could mean changing churches so they have some friends with them who are trying to follow Christ, or reading stories that would encourage them to understand that the Bible and life are related. As you do yardwork or housework, find natural ways to talk about creation and life. My relationship with God should be attractive to my children; it must be more than rules they struggle against. Finally, both spiritual and social needs can come together in a good youth group—very important during the adolescent years.

A Mom's Memory

My outgoing child tested my planning methods when she suddenly refused to go to the playground in the park. Normally, she begged every day to go play with her friends—this behavior was very unusual for her. After checking to make sure she was not sick, I made her go anyway. It was a miserable time. The second day, I gave in to her pleading and tears and kept her home.

What had happened? I started praying and using all I had learned about her from my study methods. I began to ask questions. We talked about what she liked to do at the playground, and what she didn't like to do. I discovered that she was proud and happy about certain things, and fearful of others—specifically, the monkey bars. Although they seemed to be easy for all of her little friends, she was afraid to try them, afraid she would fall. She didn't want to be embarrassed in front of her bold friends.

So what did we do? For a week, we went to the playground alone, when I knew her friends would not be around, to gain confidence on the monkey bars. After that week of practice, she was ready to enter the playground again as her usual outgoing self.

How did I know what to do in this situation? Well, at first I didn't! But I knew she had the tendency of a person who resembled the *wall*—she was like Jacob. Acceptance and success were very important to her, and if she fell off the bars she would feel like a failure. Knowing that in the past she had blamed something or someone else for her problems, or avoided them altogether, I knew that in order to be a wise steward of my child, I needed to help her face the problem and make a real effort to overcome it. After that week of practice, my daughter mastered the monkey bars and also learned that God was eager to help her learn to trust and obey Him, even at the playground.

Planning Personal Pages
4. Set aside a section of your devotional journal to be the personal pages for each of your children. Choose about two pages for each child.

a. First, paste or tape a picture of each child on one of that child's pages. This smiling face helps when we are not happy with our children's behavior. If they haven't been obedient, for instance, we may not want to pray for them. But looking at my child's picture, I am once again ready to ask God's help so I can be obedient to Him and pray as I should.

b. Second, under the picture write down any promises God has given you for your child. If you have no personal promises right now, write down any verses that God has spoken to you about from this study. These promises may be the result of what you have learned while studying your child, or comparing him or her with a person in Scripture. I pray these promises or verses every day for my children.

As your children grow, God will give you specific verses for special events in their lives. Record and date these verses. They could include when the child came to Christ, a Lordship decision, a marriage, or their own children's births. God has given me verses to pray for my grandchildren, and now I am praying for a new generation to be trained up for Him.

c. Third, on a separate page for each child, mark four columns using the Luke 2:52 guide (question 2 above). Think about these four areas of life, and record any observations you have made through the last four chapters of this study under the appropriate sections. Do this for each child on his or her page. Be sure that you update this information about every six months, as your children's needs will change. Also, make note of any steps God shows you to help train them in each area.

5. If you are meeting with a group, bring your journals with you to your group meeting. Share with the group things God has taught you as you let Him help you plan and pray for your children.

After the entire nation of Israel crossed the Jordan River into Canaan, God gave Joshua a special task. Obediently, Joshua appointed twelve men, one from each tribe as God directed. These were his words to them:

Go over before the ark of the LORD your God into the middle of Jordan. Each of you is to take up a stone on his shoulder, according to the number of the tribes of the Israelites, to serve as a sign among you. In the future, when your children ask you, "What do these stones mean?" tell them that the flow of the

Jordan was cut off before the ark of the covenant of the LORD. When it crossed the Jordan, the waters of the Jordan were cut off. These stones are to be a memorial to the people of Israel forever. (Joshua 4:5-7)

6. a. What are the "stones" in your life that represent the miracles God has worked for you personally?

b. How can you use the record in your journal as a reminder to your children of the "stones"(miracles) He has worked for them through their lives?

The things you note in your journal are like these stones from the Jordan Rivers of your life. They are concrete reminders of God's faithfulness to you. Notice that *God* told Joshua to do this, as a memorial for his generation and future generations. Both parents and children had to believe God would enable them to cross the Jordan River. The children probably realized their parents were afraid also, but they saw them walk by faith on dry land. As we commit ourselves to plan and pray using these journals, with God as our guide, our children will know that we depend on Him. Our job is to make our children thirsty to know this God who changes us, strengthens us, guides us, and provides for us. Our task is also to demonstrate by our dependence on God that He will be faithful to those who call upon Him with a sincere heart.

Long-Term Study

Plan as a habit to do some character studies on several people in Scripture, as you did on David in chapter 7. That study will take some time— don't plan to do it this week, but as you find a space when you have no other assignment to complete. List all the passages you can find about the person, from birth to death if possible. Ask yourself these questions:

&How am I like this person, and how is my child like him or her?
&What were the results of this person's actions?
&In what ways did God train him or her?
&What can I learn from this person that will apply to me or my children?

The entrance of Your words gives light;
It gives understanding to the simple.
PSALM 119:130, NKJV

Making Bible study a habit in our lives will give us greater understanding of how God works to train us and our children.

For Personal Meditation

The Lord is able to do what He will with His children, if they turn to Him and become clay in His hands, but He does not force any one of us. "Ye have not, because ye ask not," is something to be thought of in this connection. As one who has been born into God's family through coming to Him in His accepted way . . . through Christ . . . it is also necessary to turn to the Father when a "mess" has been made. To ask forgiveness? Yes, but also to ask, "Please take me and make me into what I cannot be, make me into what you now want me to be."

EDITH SCHAEFFER, *A Way of Seeing*[3]

7. Read the quote above, and think about the following questions.
   a. Are you willing to become clay in God's hands, and to let Him mold you as He pleases? Will you give your children to Him one by one for the same purpose?
   b. If you feel you have made a mess of your life, or one of your children has, will you let Him take over from this moment forward?

For Personal Prayer
Ask God to take you and make you into what you cannot be, into what God wants you to be. Ask Him to help you train each of your children as well to be who He intended them to be.

Ten

TRAIN UP A MOM:
To Let Her Children Go

❦

Blessed is the man who fears the Lord,
who finds great delight in his commands.
His children will be mighty in the land;
the generation of the upright will be blessed.
PSALM 112:1-2

This life, therefore, is not godliness but the process of
becoming godly, not health but getting well, not being, but
becoming, not rest, but exercise. We are not now what we
shall be, but we are on the way. The process is not yet
finished, but it is actively going on. This is not the goal, but it
is the right road. At present, everything does not gleam and
sparkle, but everything is being cleansed.
MARTIN LUTHER[1]

As our children become adults, we often take part in a graduation or a
wedding ceremony. With these ceremonies, we realize that our years
of direct, personal influence over our children are probably ending or
at least changing. We face the prospect of letting them go and begin to
ask ourselves several questions, such as, "Are they ready to handle the
pressures of the world?" "Have we done enough to prepare them?"
"Will they be able to handle what comes their way?" and "Will I, as their
parent, be able to entrust them to God's care and not feel driven to interfere in unwanted ways?"

All of the preceding studies have emphasized that the One who
keeps us and our children is the Lord Jesus Christ. Our relationship
with Him will sustain us, for instance, when we move into a season
when they are trying out their wings. As young adults, our children

need a different kind of care from parents. At that point we can no longer *carry* them; we must entrust them to God's plan. After all, His love and understanding for our children is crystal-clear, while ours is clouded by our fears and uncertainties about the future. We must let Him allow those things that will enable them to recognize His purpose for their lives.

Letting Them Go

Our Lord Jesus Christ also had to let His children go—His spiritual children—when He left them. When Jesus was crucified and buried, His followers grieved the end of all their dreams and hopes. After His resurrection they spent forty days with Him, and again He left them, this time to return to heaven. But He left them with the promise of the Comforter (the Holy Spirit), whom Jesus would send to stay with them forever. Still, not having Jesus' physical presence with them any longer was a real change for the disciples.

1. Read John 14:1-31.

   a. Why was it necessary for Jesus to part physically from His disciples?

   b. How did the disciples feel about His leaving them? Be specific and list verses.

   c. How is the parting between Jesus and His followers like the parting that eventually comes between a mom and her children?

   d. What happens to a child when a mother will not let him or her grow up and part from her?

   e. Can you share a time when you had to let your child go into a new stage of life? What did that feel like?

   f. What examples can you draw from this passage about letting them go?

There is a time for everything,
and a season for every activity under heaven:
a time to be born and a time to die,
a time to plant and a time to uproot.
ECCLESIASTES 3:1-2

Accepting Disappointment

2. a. In the Garden of Gethsemane, the place of Jesus' betrayal, the disciples disappointed Him in some very specific ways. Read Mark 14:32-51 and list the various ways Jesus' disciples disappointed Him.

b. What is usually your reaction when your children disappoint you by failing to do as you requested, especially when you really needed their help?

c. How have you responded when your child disappointed you by running from something difficult rather than facing it?

d. What can you learn from Jesus' response to His disciples about handling disappointment?

3. Jesus recognized His disciples' failures, but He committed Himself to pray for their future, entrusting their development to His Father. Read John 17:6-26 and list the things He prayed for them under the following categories.

love

protection

provision

4. a. What things under the category of *love* are you concerned about for your children?

b. Describe your concerns about their future *protection.*

c. List the expectations you need to commit to God for their future *provision.*

5. As you think about Jesus' attitude toward His disciples, take a moment and compare your attitude toward your children's failure with His complete acceptance of the disciples when they failed. How do you think Jesus was able to maintain this remarkable attitude toward them?

Find rest, O my soul, in God alone;
  my hope comes from him.
He alone is my rock and my salvation;
  he is my fortress, I will not be shaken.
My salvation and my honor depend on God;
  he is my mighty rock, my refuge.
Trust in him at all times, O people;
  pour out your hearts to him,
  for God is our refuge.
PSALM 62:5-8

6. a. How does this promise in Psalm 62 offer you hope for the times when your children disappoint you?

b. What responsibilities do these verses place on you as their parent?

c. How can you begin to apply these verses to your area of concern about letting your child go or accepting disappointments?

A Mom's Memory

My child's life was not going as I expected it to go! I thought that as a young adult she was making a wrong decision concerning her future. She was not making a bad decision, but I had a different picture in mind for her. A friend came to see me and as I shared my heartache, she faithfully led me to Scripture. We read John 21:15-17. In that passage, Jesus asked Peter if he loved Him with a godly love—He asked the question three times. Each time, Peter's response was, "I love you as much as I can." I was struck by Peter's response and by the fact that he was hurt when the Lord asked him yet a third time, but then I saw how the Lord responded to Peter's question. Each time, even though Peter did not love Him with a godly love, Jesus accepted what Peter could give, and gave him hope and a specific purpose. "Tend my lambs, shepherd my sheep, tend my sheep," were the words Jesus said to him. Jesus did not wait for Peter to have the perfect response before accepting him and giving him reassurance (John 21:15-17, NASB).

As I worked on this passage, God showed me my unaccepting heart! I was not accepting my child and trusting God with her decision. I was holding out for what I wanted before I would give her my blessing. I was grieving her by not giving her any hope in God's plan for her life. I confessed my sin to God and asked my daughter's forgiveness as well. Then, together, we embraced her plans with great joy, trusting God for her future.

How grateful I was for that faithful friend. How grateful I was for God's work in my heart. Many years later I know that the path my daughter chose was in exact keeping with God's purpose for her life. *I* wanted to do God's work, instead of letting *Him* do it. I let my disappointment interfere with my acceptance of God's purpose for her future.

7. Remember the story of Isaac and Rebekah? Let's look at it again from the perspective of acceptance. As Isaac was nearing death, he called his oldest son, Esau, to him and gave him some instruction. Read Genesis 27:1-4.

   a. What did Isaac tell Esau to do?

   b. What do you think this desire for himself suggests about Isaac's acceptance of his son?

   c. What could have happened if Isaac had blessed Esau without wanting something for himself first?

   d. What do we have to do for Jesus before He will accept us and confer His blessing on us?

8. Think about your children individually. In what area might you be withholding acceptance or love because your child has not performed according to your expectations? Write down areas God brings to mind and ask for grace to make the necessary changes.

But as many as received Him, to them He gave the right to become children of God, even to those who believe in His name.
JOHN 1:12, NASB

Leaving a Spiritual Inheritance

Perhaps you, like I, do not come from an inheritance of a long line of people who walked with God. If that is the case for you, rejoice that God has done a new thing in your family. After several generations of neglect for God's principles, He started a new beginning with your family.

When I think of the tangible resources that our children might inherit, they do not provide much security. But when I think of the spiritual resources God in His grace has given as a foundation, I have much for which to be thankful. One of our daughters wrote these words in her love letter to her father:

> I have seen you trust the Lord through different positions, differ-ent homes, different states, and you have been graced by Him in each place. I pray that my life will someday have even a small dose of your experience in trusting the Lord for all answers to life. I really admire you in that God has given you so many promises, and you have had a long time to trust Him. I pray that one day I will be able to have the trust you possess in our Lord.

Even if my daughter receives a small tangible inheritance, this desire for a large spiritual inheritance is expressing itself in her adult life today, and God is honoring her desire as she continues to seek Him.

9. Ephesians 1 tells us about our inheritance as children of God in Jesus Christ. Read aloud Eugene Peterson's paraphrase of that chap-ter (see below), and consider the inheritance you have received if you belong to Jesus.

How blessed is God! And what a blessing He is! He's the Father of our Master, Jesus Christ, and takes us to the high places of blessing in him. Long before he laid down earth's foundations, he had us in mind, had settled on us as the focus of his love, to be made whole and holy by his love. Long, long ago he decided to adopt us into his family through Jesus Christ. (What pleasure he took in planning this!) He wanted us to enter into the cele-bration of his lavish gift-giving by the hand of his beloved Son.

Because of the sacrifice of the Messiah, his blood poured out on the altar of the Cross, we're a free people—free of penalties and punishments chalked up by all our misdeeds. And not just barely free, either. Abundantly free! He thought of everything, provided for everything we could possibly need, letting us in on the plans he took such delight in making. He set it all before us in Christ, a long-range plan in which everything would be brought together and summed up in him, everything in deepest heaven, everything on planet earth.

It's in Christ that we find out who we are and what we are liv-ing for. Long before we first heard of Christ and got our hopes up, he had his eye on us, had designs on us for glorious living, part of the overall purpose he is working out in everything and everyone. (Ephesians 1:3-11, MSG)

10.a. From the passage above, list all that Paul says you have received from Jesus.

b. Now list what God longs to give you in the future.

11. Review the two lists you made in response to the preceding question. Ask yourself the following questions concerning your children and their next step in life.

a. Do I believe that God loves my children more than I ever could?
b. Does God understand their needs better than I?
c. Is God able to change their hearts when I can't?
d. Can God do for them things they will not allow me to do?
e. Will I believe God and trust His plan for my children as they take the next step?

For Personal Meditation

At a parade, a strong father is often seen picking up a little child and carrying her on his shoulders. Perhaps it's to enable her to see better, to protect her from the crowds below, or to give her some rest if she's tired from trying to keep up with Dad. Sitting on her dad's shoulders, she doesn't have a care at all. She could see forever and go everywhere her father goes regardless of the crowds.

I am reminded of Deuteronomy 1:31: "There you saw how the LORD your God carried you, as a father carries his son." God gives us the privilege, the joy, and the responsibility of carrying our children until they reach adulthood, and it is sometimes hard to let them down from that position of security. When our children are on our shoulders, we can protect them and take them only where we want them to go. But when they grow up, they no longer fit on our shoulders.

As they become adults, we love them as deeply as when they were dependent on us. But the carrying is now transferred to the strong shoulders of the Lord Jesus Christ. This transfer is an ongoing process, a step at a time. Our children may even try to get back on our shoulders, and missing the companionship this closeness afforded, we may take them back. But as the Ephesians passage so clearly says, God has the road all figured out for each of them. Our task is to let Him have them, entrust them to His care, be available when they need us, and pray, pray, pray.

12. Consider the way you answered question 11. What do your answers tell you about your readiness to let your children take their next step in life? What will you do to better prepare yourself for this next step? Be specific for each child.

For Personal Prayer

Carefree, she stepped into the sunlight, her face uplifted
    to the sun;
while I, aware of brewing storms that etched the sky,
clutched at a fear and nursed it.
Then I saw her hand outstretched like a small child;
and while I watched, Another Hand reached down
    and clasped it.
I heard the distant thunder with a smile.
RUTH BELL GRAHAM, *Sitting by My Laughing Fireplace*[2]

Commit each of your children to the spiritual inheritance He desires for them. Pray that each of them will stretch out their hands to let Him clasp it. Ask Him to help you smile at the future as you entrust them to His hands.

Notes

Preface
1. Rodlyn Danos, *Lead the Way*, unpublished poem. Used by permission.

Chapter One—Train up a Mom: To Want to Grow
1. C. S. Lewis, *Mere Christianity* (New York, NY: Macmillan Publishing Co., Inc.,1960), p. 75.
2. Ruth Bell Graham, *Sitting by My Laughing Fire Place* (Montreat, N. C.: BGEA,1977), p. 114. Used by permission.
3. David B. Guralnik, *Webster's New World Dictionary* (Eaglewood Cliffs, NJ: Prentice-Hall, Inc., 1968), p. 1131.
4. Guralnik, p. 1568.
5. Guralnik, p. 90.

Chapter Two—Train up a Mom:To Walk in Intimacy
1. Oswald Chambers, *My Utmost for His Highest*. Edited by James Reimann, (1992 by Oswald Chambers Publications Association, Ltd.) Original edition 1935 by Dodd, Mead & Co., renewed 1963 by the Oswald Chambers Publications Association, Ltd., (Grand Rapids, MI: Discovery House Publishers). Devotional from July 20. Used by permission.
2. Shirley Gupton Lynn, *The Opening*, compiled by Karen Greenwaldt in *For Everything There is a Season*. Volume Title: *A Guide to Prayer for All People* (Nashville, TN: Upper Room Books, 1990), p. 150. Used by permission.
3. J. Oswald Sanders, original source unknown.
4. Henry T. Blackaby and Claude V. King, *Experiencing God* (Nashville, TN: Lifeway Press, 1990), p. 44.

Chapter Three—Train up a Mom:To Accept God's Way
1. Charles R. Swindoll, *Growing Wise in Family Life* (retitled *The Strong Family*), (1988 by Charles R. Swindoll. Used by permission of Zondervan Publishing House, Grand Rapids, MI), p. 99.
2. Patricia Daniels Cornwell, *Time for Remembering, The Story of Ruth Bell Graham* (New York, NY: Harper & Row Publishers, Inc., 1983), p. 140.
3. Chambers, *My Utmost for His Highest*. Devotional from April 29.

Chapter Four—Train up a Mom:To Walk by Faith
1. Charles Colson, *Loving God* (Grand Rapids, MI: Zondervan Publishing House, 1983), p. 38.
2. Swindoll, *Growing Wise in Family Life*, p. 40.

Chapter Five—Train up a Mom:To Love Supernaturally
1. Chambers, *My Utmost for His Highest*. Devotional from April 30.
2. Edith Schaeffer, *What Is a Family?* (Old Tappan, NJ: Fleming H. Revell Co. , 1975), p. 89.
3. Guralnik, *Webster's New World Dictionary*, p. 1429.

Chapter Six—Train up a Mom:To Study Her Children
1. Swindoll, *Growing Wise in Family Life*, p. 69.

Chapter Seven—Train up a Mom:To Affirm Their Natural Bent
1. Story of the Potter, original source unknown.

Chapter Eight—Train up a Mom:To Claim God's Promises
1. Ray C. Stedman, *Life, the Teacher* Discovery Papers, Catalog No. 3024, series title: *Guidelines for the Home* (Palo Alto, CA: Discovery Publishers, 1973).
2. Guralnik, *Webster's New World Dictionary*, p. 1137.
3. Guralnik, p. 1130.
4. W. E. Vine, M.A. *Vine's Expository Dictionary of Biblical Words* (Nashville, Camden, NY: Thomas Nelson Publishers, 1984), p. 491.
5. Graham, *Sitting by My Laughing Fireplace*, p. 154.

Chapter Nine—Train up a Mom:To Pray and Plan
1. Jean Fleming, *A Mother's Heart* (Colorado Springs, CO: NavPress, 1982, revised 1996), p. 91.
2. Schaeffer, *What Is a Family?*, p. 170.
3. Edith Schaeffer, *A Way Of Seeing* (Old Tapan, NJ: Fleming H. Revell Company, 1977), p. 78.

Chapter Ten—Train up a Mom: To Let Her Children Go
1. Martin Luther, original source unknown.
2. Graham, *Sitting by My Laughing Fireplace*, p. 146.

Author

VOLLIE SANDERS is the mother of three, the grandmother of four, and the "spiritual mother" of many who have lived in the home of her and her husband, Darrell. She is a free-lance writer, having written many Bible studies used in churches and with individuals, and a popular speaker at women's groups and conferences. Vollie has recently been named the director for women's ministries for The Navigators.

Vollie and Darrell have served on staff with The Navigators for 26 years, in Florida, Tennessee, and California. They currently live in Colorado Springs, Colorado.

Just for Mom

HOMEMAKING

Women today work to fulfill a variety of roles—mother, friend, spouse, employee. This Bible study will help you discover what it means to be a woman made in God's image and how to nurture your family in today's world.

Homemaking
(Tjitske Lemstra & Baujke Doornenbal) $7

•

MOTHERS HAVE ANGEL WINGS

This collection of stories about the joys and trials of motherhood will inspire, encourage, and challenge you as you explore specific biblical principles related to being a mom.

Mothers Have Angel Wings
(Carol Kent) $12

•

A MOTHER'S HEART

Being a mother is an important job, but one that can easily feel frustrating and unrewarding. This book will help you learn to become the mother God designed you to be.

A Mother's Heart
(Jean Fleming) $9

Get your copies today at your local bookstore, through our website, or by calling (800) 366-7788. Ask for offer **#2237** or a FREE catalog of NavPress resources.

NAVPRESS
BRINGING TRUTH TO LIFE
w w w . n a v p r e s s . c o m

Prices subject to change.